Enneagram and Chakras

Modern Day Enneagram Discovery of Yourself
and Others Through Personality Types

(Personality Types and All Subtypes Explained and
Learn How to Have Better Relationships)

Michael Holoman

Published by Knowledge Icons

Michael Holoman

All Rights Reserved

Enneagram and Chakras: Modern Day Enneagram Discovery of Yourself and Others Through Personality Types (Personality Types and All Subtypes Explained and Learn How to Have Better Relationships)

ISBN 978-1-990084-49-2

All rights reserved. No part of this guide may be reproduced in any form without permission in writing from the publisher except in the case of brief quotations embodied in critical articles or reviews.

Legal & Disclaimer

The information contained in this book is not designed to replace or take the place of any form of medicine or professional medical advice. The information in this book has been provided for educational and entertainment purposes only.

The information contained in this book has been compiled from sources deemed reliable, and it is accurate to the best of the Author's knowledge; however, the Author cannot guarantee its accuracy and validity and cannot be held liable for any errors or omissions. Changes are periodically made to this book. You must consult your doctor or get professional medical advice before using any of the suggested remedies, techniques, or information in this book.

Upon using the information contained in this book, you agree to hold harmless the Author from and against any damages, costs, and expenses, including any legal fees potentially resulting from the application of any of the information provided by this guide. This disclaimer applies to any damages or injury caused by the use and application, whether directly or indirectly, of any advice or information presented, whether for breach of contract, tort, negligence, personal injury, criminal intent, or under any other cause of action.

You agree to accept all risks of using the information presented inside this book. You need to consult a professional medical practitioner in order to ensure you are both able and healthy enough to participate in this program.

Table of Contents

INTRODUCTION 1

CHAPTER 1: IDENTIFYING YOUR PERSONALITY TYPE 2

CHAPTER 2: WHAT IS EMOTIONAL INTELLIGENCE 13

CHAPTER 3: READING THE ENNEAGRAM 19

CHAPTER 4: THE HELPER (TYPE 2) 31

CHAPTER 5: THE TRIADS, THE HEART AND SOUL OF THE ENNEAGRAM 46

CHAPTER 6: THE JAPANESE RESTAURANT STORY 67

CHAPTER 7: WHY CHOOSE ENNEAGRAM AND WHAT ARE THE BENEFITS YOU CAN GET FROM IT? 84

CHAPTER 8: SUBTYPES IN ENNEAGRAM 96

CHAPTER 9: TYPE THREE - THE PERFORMER 115

CHAPTER 10: ENNEAGRAM TYPE 2 128

CHAPTER 11: HOW TO CHOOSE CAREER PATH AND A PARTNER BASED ON THE KIND OF PERSONALITY 138

CHAPTER 12: THE INVESTIGATOR 155

CHAPTER 13: ENNEA-TYPE SIX – "THE LOYALIST" 170

CHAPTER 14: ENNEAGRAM TYPE 7 - THE DREAMER/EPICURE 185

CONCLUSION 191

Introduction

To belong to yourself is to fully know who you are, and still manage to show and your flaws to the world in all their glory. It's not about being fatalistic and just accepting things as they are. It's about being fully secure with your knowledge of yourself, and as a direct consequence, being able to trust in your own decisions and stick to your principles. In the most motherly of tones, it's about being yourself.

It's not about dreaming to be as athletic as Lebron James, or as smart as Albert Einstein, or as wealthy as Bill Gates. It's about understanding that you truly can live your dreams but that you can't have everything. Because no one actually has everything – no one ever had it and no one ever will. And you will see the truth to this philosophy through the enneagram, a tool that is used to jumpstart self-awareness.

Chapter 1: Identifying Your Personality Type

Identifying Your Personality Type on Your Own

There's one thing to remember when typing yourself and others – there really is no grand secret to it. You simply have to know about the traits that go with each type as well as the behaviors that result from such traits.

Make no mistake, analysis takes a lot of nuance because there are so many quirks to each personality type, and human beings are complex and layered.

Avoid focusing too much on one trait. Note that one trait could appear in different types. However, how people manifest those traits could differ. For example, empathy in a Helper is brought by the need to love and be loved, whereas a Peacemaker being considerate is brought by the need to maintain harmony. Here's another example: Reformers tend to defy the rules because they want something better. Challengers tend to defy the rules because they don't respect rules. Try to see each type in its entirety – including fears and desires.In addition, learn all you can about the other types, especially those that are traditional wings to what you deem to be your basic type.

Converse with people and reach out to the Enneagram community. We have so much to learn from other people. We all share the human experience at a certain level. The stories that other people share about their journey and experiences can help you find out the mystery of your true self.

Enneagram Typing and Tests

This book was designed to give you a starting point toward finding out who you really are. With the help of the information, you are able to generate report on your behaviors, beliefs, and attitudes, and that would have been the data you use to type yourself. There is, however, a problem with self-reported data – the data that you yourself have collected about you.

The Pitfalls of Using Self-Reported Data

Self-reported data is frequently used in psychological studies, of which personality analysis is a part, primarily because the information is easy to obtain. In fact, clinicians use self-reported data to an extent in order to make the right diagnosis – they ask questions. The main problem with self-reported data is that it has its limitations, such as the following:

Social Desirability Concerns

You might not want to admit certain undesirable traits about yourself so you refuse to acknowledge them, resulting to inaccurate data.

Question Order Bias

Overtime, as the subject may react differently depending on the other of in which the questions appeared.

Introspective Ability

Some subjects lack the ability required to properly evaluate themselves. They might not be able to connect the dots or miss important things entirely.

Problems

With the Interpretation of the questions – In some cases, the subject finds the wording of the questions confusing. Some people may also take a certain word differently.

Interpretation of the questions

The wording of the questions may be confusing or have different meanings to different subjects.

Enneagram Typing Programs and Centers

Self-report data should not be the sole source of data if your goal is to be as accurate as possible. This isn't to say you shouldn't ever use self-reported data.

However, it should be used in conjunction with other information such as the individual's actual behavior.

Third parties are not as close to you so they may be able to spot response biases. They have access to tools such as specially designed questionnaires that have been evaluated to make sure that they can produce consistent results over time.

You can always try the Enneagram tests you see online for fun, but don't forget that they may not always give accurate results due to the limitations of self-reported data. Some of them have been developed by Enneagram community members who have also just begun their journey.

There are, however, reliable enneagram testing programs and centers that could give you accurate results.

1. David Daniel's Stanford Enneagram Discovery and Inventory Guide is one of the most popular tests and is another good option.

2. One of the best ways to get a formal assessment is through Wagner Enneagram Personality Style Scales. It's the only Enneagram typing test that's included in the 2003 Mental measurements yearbook, which is published by The Buros Center for testing, a nonprofit organization formed with the goal of providing critical appraisals of tests in order to improve testing, assessment, and measurement standards and practices in the field of consultation and education, particularly in the field of psychology.

It's not a series of questions but a short description of the nine paragraph types. This test requires self-observation; it requires you to play an active role in recalling and observing your own behavioral patterns and tendencies. Based on the descriptions of the types, choose the three that seem to fit you best, and then rank them accordingly. Your basic type is likely the highest ranking and the other are your wings.

3. You can also get your type through the Narrative Tradition technique. It's a scientifically validated online version of the test in David Daniel's Essential Enneagram work.

It also comprises three parts. First, you will be shown short paragraphs that describe each type and as you read each one, determine if it describes you as a whole. Then, create a short list of the types you feel you belong to. The final step entails reviewing the similarities and differences of the types in your short list. After introspection and self-observation, you might be able to pinpoint the type that you likely belong to. Check their core fears and desires to see if they match yours.

If you join the Narrative Tradition program, you'll be able to access videos and explore themes, motivations, coping strategies, and paths to growth.

4. The Enneagram Institute's Riso-Hudson Enneagram Type Indicator is also accurate. When answered properly, Enneagram

indicator questionnaires can identify your basic personality type. It's a scientifically validated, forced choice test with 144 paired statements. It can take up to 40 minutes to complete. This test is pretty comprehensive, producing a full spectrum profile that gives you insights on all the nine types that may be within your overall personality.

How to Get Accurate Results When Taking an Enneagram Test?

There are a few things to keep in mind when taking any Enneagram test to ensure that you get accurate results.

1, Make sure to answer the questions honestly. Ask yourself these questions before choosing an answer:

Is that really how you are?

Are you sure it's not just something you'd like to be?

Is that something you have tended to do so or to be in the past?

The answers to all those questions should be 'yes'.

It's difficult to answer many of the questions honestly because it's human nature to want to see themselves as better than they are. That's why the Dunning-Kruger effect is so prevalent in human beings.

2. Keep in mind that your self-image is not your true image. We tend to have preconceived notions about ourselves, some of which aren't true at all.

For example, you like to think of yourself as a naturally generous person, but it could be that your generosity is an effort to curb your fears of maintaining harmony. You tend to give way so much that you end up resentful but you do not believe that you truly are resentful.

To get accurate results from your Enneagram analysis, keep these natural tendencies in mind.

3. It might help to try to look from the outside.

When answering questions, consider if the answer you've chosen is how someone close to you would describe you as well.

After Getting the Results

There is one thing you should not stop doing after getting your results – learning. Find out more about your Type and examine the other types that also seem to be dominant in you.

Enneagram tests generally generate a report in which you get a score for each pf the nine types. Scoring the highest in a particular category indicates that you are likely dominant in that category. Learn more about the top three categories in which you got the highest scores.

More importantly, try to listen to other people's stories. Listen to what they have to say about their own journey to self-discovery. Learn about how a certain type lives his life, and how they cope with life's challenges. We can always learn from each other.

Sooner or later, you will see there is a pattern to everything – every action has its corresponding reaction and each one of is affected by the other.

Chapter 2: What Is Emotional Intelligence

In 1995, renowned psychologist and scientific journalist Daniel Goleman published a book introducing the emerging concept of emotional intelligence to the world. He presented EI as the ability to understand and manage one's emotions which greatly increases one's potential for success and this proposition was welcomed by a world that's growingly thirsty for self-actualization. The concept of emotional intelligence rapidly went on to influence the way people think about emotions and human behavior.

In an article on EI framework published by Salovey and Mayer, emotional intelligence has been defined "as a set of skills hypothesized to contribute to the accurate appraisal and expression of emotion in oneself and in others, the effective regulation of emotion in self and others, and the use of feelings to motivate, plan, and achieve in one's life."[3]

Emotional intelligence refers to how well you are able to manage your emotions, as well as of others'. Amid debates among psychology scholars over what really constitutes emotional intelligence, there is a general agreement that EI consists of at least three skills. These are emotional awareness; the ability to harness one's emotions and leveraging on them in completing tasks such as critical thinking or problem-solving; and the ability to regulate one's own emotions when necessary.

The term "emotional intelligence" (with abbreviations EI or EQ for emotional quotient) was penned by researchers Peter Salavey and John Mayer. The concept was further popularized by Goleman in a book of the same name in 1995. EI is the ability to recognize, understand, and manage one's emotions. EI also includes the ability to recognize and influence the emotions of others. This awareness of our emotions can drive our behavior and can affect people, in both positive and negative ways. This is why learning how to manage emotions – our own and others' – has come to be crucial, most particularly when we are under certain conditions of pressure.

Be aware, though, that EI is an entirely separate principle from Personality. A person's personality is more constant throughout an individual's lifetime, whereas EI is more pliable and can be enhanced, in spite of not being inherently born with it.

In an article by Dr. Travis Bradberry ("Why You Need Emotional Intelligence"), he explained that there have been findings that individuals with average IQs outperform those with the highest IQs 70% of the time. This peculiarity put into question the traditional assumption that intelligence was the sole predictor for success. Years of research now are pointing to a "missing link" – emotional intelligence – which is more critical in setting top performing individuals apart from the rest.

In simpler terms, EI is the "X Factor" ... that "something" intangible in each of us that describes how we manage behavior, how we navigate through complex social intricacies, and how we make decisions that bring about maximum positive returns.

You may have observed, too, that the Top 3 in your highschool class years ago are not necessarily the most successful or the most fulfilled now that you are in your adult lives. You probably know at least one person who was academically outstanding but is socially awkward or possibly frustrated in their careers or personal relationships. One's intelligence quotient (IQ) is not the be-all, end-all indicator of a person's potential for success. Sure, a high IQ might help you get into the college of your choice. But it's your EI that will help you abundantly in managing all the stress and high-level emotions when you are about to take the final exams.

Emotional intelligence is connected to a basic element of human behavior that is separate from intellect. There is no established connection between IQ and EI; these two concepts are in no direct correlation to one another. In other words, how smart someone is will not be indicative of how emotionally intelligent that same person is. Your intelligence is your ability to learn and it is the same when you were 16 as it will be when you're 65. On the other hand, EI is a versatile skill set that can be acquired and improved with consistent practice throughout your life.

Another piece that completes the puzzle that is human behavior is personality. It is the constant "style" that defines a person. An individual's personality hails from his or her genetic preferences, such as the propensity for either extroversion or introversion. Very much like IQ, one's personality is stable and constant throughout his or her lifetime and is not a predictor for emotional intelligence.

Chapter 3: Reading The Enneagram

Once you have finished an Enneagram test, you are likely eager to interpret the results. You will want to know exactly what it can tell you in order to begin moving forward with your newfound understanding of who you are as a person.As you read through this chapter, you will be guided through understanding the results clearly, as well as the benefits you can gain from the insight gathered after having completed an Enneagram test for yourself. Keep in mind that at this point, you have taken either one or several tests and are ready to start understanding what the results mean.

Enneagram Test Results

Your results will provide you with several important points—you will be looking for the basic type, the wings, and the directions of integration and disintegration based on the number that you will gain. It is also important to keep in mind that you may have several results that are close together, and in that case, you will have to figure out which is the primary type for you.

Basic or Primary Type

The basic type is usually the most obvious—it is the highest score on your Enneagram test. This is usually by a significant margin (at least 4 points) compared to the second and third highest scores. If they are closer than 4 points apart, then it is possible that you will have to figure out which one is more in tune with who you are as an individual.

When you have taken your test, you should look at the top three scores—especially if you are a woman who has just scored highly in a 2, you may want to consider other options as well. All too often, women are taught to play the Helper role without it being a basic type for them. They are taught to consider the needs of others before their own to a fault, though they may really belong within another type altogether.

Read the three highest scores you got in the following chapters and pick which aligns closest to you. If you are still unsure after reading the descriptions, you could always try spending a week or so reflecting on your own behaviors actively, spending the time to consciously identify what you are doing as you do it in order to gain insight into what your true type may be.

Wings

At this point, you should know what your basic type is. Now, it is time to look at your wings—the surrounding scores and how they are relevant to you. At this point, take a moment to look at the surrounding scores. If you scored a 3, for example, you will be looking specifically at your wings of 2 and 4. Determine which score was higher on your results—this wing will be your dominant wing. For example, if your wing of 2 scored higher than your wing of 4, then your 2 wing would be dominant.

Of course, you will also need to note how high or low your score is. If both of your wings scores are quite low, it is possible that neither wing is dominant at all. If both scores are equal and higher, then it is possible that both wings are dominant and relevant to you.

Directions of Integration and Disintegration

It will also be important to give close consideration to your directions of integration and disintegration. These are the relaxation or stress responses. In general, these directions of integration will also have relatively high scores in comparison to others.

What to Do When Results Are Close?

When the results are close, it is important to figure out which is the most accurate. This means that you will need to look at your scores closely in a wide range of scenarios. Read each of the results to see if you can relate to any more than the others just through going over them. It is possible that, after reading, you will know which one is more likely to be your basic type. If not, you can start to look at wings and directions of integration and disintegration. Usually, you will see higher numbers on the wings and on the directions of integration and disintegration than on the other scores, so if you compare your close results at all points, you should be able to identify one that has higher scores than others. You can also try taking the test again in the future after a few days, or try taking a test under a different teacher to see if you get any further information.

Steps to Understanding Enneagram Test Results When They Are Unclear

Sometimes, despite your best efforts, you cannot tell your score still. If this is your dilemma after having taken a test, try following the following steps. It is likely that you will gain some sort of insight through following these that will help you in the future.

Start by looking at your top three scores. One of these three will most likely be your basic type, so you can focus your attention on these instead of having nine different types to parse through in order to figure yourself out.

In regards to those three, start to consider how you grew up. Did you grow up with a certain culture? Or perhaps, you grew up in an environment that dictated certain behaviors to be upheld in order to avoid trouble. For example, women tend to score highly in Type 2 personality types thanks to stereotypes regarding women. If you can see a relation between one of your highest scores and your upbringing, it is entirely possible that this type is not your basic personality type, despite the fact that it is a part of you.

Next, compare your directions of integration and disintegration and the wings—you will most likely have a high score on one of those. If one of your top three scores also connects to highly scored wings and directions of integration and disintegration, it is likely your basic type.

Keep in mind that ultimately, only you can determine our personality type. You will know your personality type when you read it—it will resonate deeply within you, and you will know it when you see it. Follow your own intuition when trying to figure it out—it should steer you in the right direction.

Benefits of Enneagram

When you do finally read through your enneagram type and start to understand it and who you are as an individual, you will start to see the benefits. You will be able to acknowledge your strengths and weaknesses. You will be able to use your newfound knowledge to help you improve your relationships with those around you. You will also understand yourself and therefore find that you are largely happier than you were before thanks to that understanding and self-awareness that it brought with it.

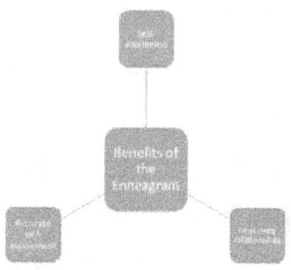

Understanding Strengths and Weaknesses

Perhaps one of the best benefits will be being able to acknowledge your own strengths and weaknesses. Think about it—when you know what you are strong at, you will be able to start utilizing that. You will be able to make it a point to utilize those strengths. Perhaps you feel like it is time for a career change—knowing your strengths and personality type will help you make the best possible choice. Perhaps you find that you are getting into arguments frequently—you will be able to figure out how to use your strengths attributed to your personality type to stop those arguments in their track.

Understanding strengths and weaknesses is a particularly useful skill—in fact, it is a foundational skill in emotional intelligence. When you are self-aware enough to understand your own abilities, you are able to ensure that you are always acting within them. You are making it a point to use your strengths to your best advantage and utilizing your weaknesses as well. Think about it this way—if you know that you struggle with conflict resolution, or with leading other people, you are not likely to put yourself in a position where you are responsible for either of them. You know that you struggle in those aspects, so you protect yourself from having to go through with them in the first place. You also know that you can work on those particular weaknesses in order to keep them from hurting you. If you are able to better yourself to strengthen those weaknesses, you are engaging in self-betterment that could be absolutely essential to you.

Improving Relationships

Another crucial benefit form learning your Enneagram type is discovering how you will interact with other people. If you know the type of your partner or close friends, you will be able to tell just how compatible or incompatible you are based on your personality scores. When you understand how you behave in a relationship and are also able to consider how your partner also behaves, you can start to see where conflicts are regularly arising. In understanding that, you can start to make the necessary changes to avoid having those issues in the future. You will be able to strengthen your relationships with those necessary changes, and with those changes, you will find that you are happier and more fulfilled.

Understanding the Self

The last crucial element here is you develop an understanding of yourself. You see exactly who you are once and for all, and in doing so, you come to develop a healthy appreciation for who you are. You will know when you are at your best or at your worst based on your actions as they are happening, and in knowing that, in being able to cue into your true mental state, you can make the changes necessary. For example, if you can see that you are starting to act in accordance with your direction of disintegration, you can correct that. If you see that your behaviors are becoming unhealthy for you, you can start to make necessary changes.

Since each and every personality type will come with its own state of health, ranging from healthy, to average, to unhealthy, you will know what to look for. In seeing those red flags, you can keep yourself from spiraling before things get truly bad. In being able to keep yourself from spiraling, you will find yourself happier in general.

Overall, learning your personality type will remove the shroud of mystery behind who you are. You will have a healthier appreciation for who you are as a person. This is essential for you— as you discover and understand who you are, understanding your fears and ideals, as well as what you desire or could be tempted by, you will start to use this to your advantage. If you know that you have a tendency toward anger, you can use that anger constructively, for example. You can use it as motivation to get the change you need rather than to punish the object of your anger. If you know that you are motivated by integrity, you can seek to keep your behaviors pure.

From this point on, every chapter will focus on providing you with a thorough overview of each and every Enneagram type. You will get all of the basic information, identifying the holy ideas, fears, desires, temptations, passions, and virtues. You will discover the directions of integration and disintegration, and see what each of these personality types can bring to their relationships. Lastly, you will get an overview of the strengths and weaknesses each of these Enneagram types bring with them.

Chapter 4: The Helper (Type 2)

Also known as the Giver

Fifteen Signs You're a Helper

You love to be involved in other people's lives.

You always feel the urge to put other people before yourself.

You tend to give a lot of time and money to charity.

You are able to see the good in your fellow humans.

You need to be needed.

You can totally exhaust yourself, running around doing things for other people.

You may feel offended if someone refuses your offer of help.

You require appreciation for the things you do for others.

Your friends describe you as being someone who is always willing to go that extra mile.

You sometimes forget to look after yourself and this can lead to physical or emotional burnout.

You don't consider life worth living unless you are giving to others in some way.

You have a deep seated fear of worthlessness.

You might well be a wonderful cook and homemaker!

You might have a tendency to use food to 'stuff' down your feelings.

Personal relationships are of the utmost importance to you.

Do any of the above points ring a bell?

The Helper: An Overview

The focus of Type Two of the Enneagram is very much on relationships. It is what makes these people tick - making connections and then empathizing with the feelings and needs of others. However, they can go too far in this tendency and can twist themselves into all sorts of shapes just to win approval from their peers. Co-dependency is a trap that type two can sometimes fall prey to, priding themselves on what they can do for other people and feeling shame at those times when they can't actually help or support others.

In a way, our culture nurtures and awards the typical behavior of a Type Two, in that it encourages us to believe that our self-worth comes from what we do for other people. Women especially are taught this kind of behaviour. Although being kind to others is, of course, laudable, the Helper must guard against a tendency to smother or overwhelm. And it is never good for someone to deny their own personal interests and needs. Burnout or martyrdom may ensue! So if you are a Two, you would do well to balance your impulse to assist others with your own self-care.

As a Helper, love is your highest goal. You pride yourself on selflessness. You are often extroverted and may also have the knack for creating a comfortable and welcoming home for your family. You are huge on empathy and often a genuinely caring person with a very warm heart. You are friendly and generous. Just make sure that your motives for helping others are pure.

Examples of famous twos include such luminaries as Bishop Desmond Tutu, Byron Katie, John Denver, Dolly Parton, Eleanor Roosevelt, Luciano Pavarotti, Stevie Wonder, Elizabeth Taylor, Martin Sheen, Bobby McFerrin, Lionel Richie, Nancy Reagan, Josh Groban, Paula Abdul and Barry Manilow.

Type two has been given the name 'The Helper' for a reason: these people are either the most genuinely helpful to others **or** the most in need to see themselves as helpful.

The Helper Levels

As with every other type, Helpers differ in maturity and psychological health. We will explore the state of The Helper at healthy, neutral and unhealthy stages.

Healthy

Unconditionally Loving

The Helper at his or her best is capable of giving truly unconditional love. He or she is humble and unselfish, feeling it is a privilege to give and to be meaningfully involved in the lives of others.

Empathetic

Empathy is the helper's middle name. This type can be spilling over with compassion and concern for their fellow human beings. In addition, they have learnt the art and value of forgiveness.

Encouraging

The Helper at this level can easily appreciate the goodness of other people. They have learnt to balance service with self-care and give for all the right reasons.

Neutral

The People-Pleaser

An air of desperation can sometimes creep into Type Two's desire to help others. A kind of clinging rather than closeness. They might be tempted to give compliments that are not entirely genuine but instead meant to gain favor from the person they are flattering.

The Co-Dependent

This stage involves possessiveness and intrusiveness. The need to be needed can become so strong that the Type Two can be deeply controlling yet tell themselves that they are actually being loving. They want others to be dependent on them and often wear themselves out with needlessly self-sacrificial behaviour.

Self-Importance

A heightened sense of self-importance is probable at this level. Martyrdom can really kick in with the Helper believing that they are being far more helpful than they actually are! Type Two at this level might feel that he or she is indispensable when they are really not, and this can cause them to be patronizing and overbearing.

Unhealthy

Manipulation

Oh dear! Things start to get nasty when Type Twos exhibit unhealthy behavior patterns. At this level, a Two may well pile on the guilt, highlighting how much they believe people owe them for all they've done. This level displays the general attitude of "How **could** you after everything I've done for you?!" If people do not show the requisite level of appreciation, they might undermine them in an aggressive way. At this level, the Two will lack the self-awareness to see how unreasonable and damaging their behavior is. They may also begin to use food and drugs as a way of self-medication.

Domineering

At this unsavory level, the Two feels that everybody they've "helped" - whether or not that person asked for that help in the first place or actually wanted it at all! - owes them an enormous debt of gratitude and therefore must "pay" in whatever way the Two deems appropriate. There is a negative sense of entitlement where this type asserts the hold they feel they have earned.

Chronic Resentment

Such resentment arises when an unhealthy Two steps fully into victim mode and feels unjustly abused by those they have "helped." Because of this, they feel justified in displaying all sorts of irrational and aggressive behavior. All these highly negative emotions can result in serious health problems, both physical and mental. Not a happy place to be! Both for the Helper and for those around them.

The Helper Wings

As previously discussed, a type's wings are derived from the two number types that are physically beside it on the circumference of the Enneagram figure. For the Helper, the Reformer (Type 1) and the Achiever (Type 3) are possible wings or influencers on the personality.

Type Two with a One Wing (2W1)

We have already seen that Type Ones are perfectionists at heart. On the plus side, they are responsible, conscientious, progress-oriented and potentially heroic. Their shadow side can be hyper-critical, this being directed both at themselves and others. At times, they can also be resentful and judgemental. So what can a Type Two with a One wing look like?

All going well, this combination of types leads to a person who is loving, warm and generous, as you would expect, but the One influence adds resolve and moral obligation. The desire to do good is thus heightened by the number One's motivation to do everything 'right.'

The focus of the One's generosity becomes a drive for social justice under the influence of the Reformer. The desire to improve the world is genuine. The Helper with this wing is also more willing to take on the unglamorous tasks that other people usually eschew, for the sake of the common good. The influence of the One on the Two can imbue them with a stronger backbone and a better awareness of where feelings might threaten to overtake their good judgment.

But, as always, there is a flip side. Destructive perfectionism could rear its ugly head, causing the helper to think that they, and they alone, know best. This makes them imposing, preachy and intrusive. They may also judge themselves very severely. A potential negative side of this combination of types can also be that the Two has even more trouble recognizing her own needs and feelings and strongly believes that her own personal desire is selfish and should be quashed.

Type Two with a Three Wing (1W3)

We will examine Type Three in detail later on. For the time being, here is a brief summary:

Type Three is variously known as the Achiever or the Performer. As the name suggests, these people tend to be ambitious, enthusiastic and adaptable. They are driven and like nothing more than to accomplish goals and receive validation from others.

A Three wing makes the Two more social and good-humored than a One wing tends to do. It is all about the heart and feelings when it comes to this pairing. Relationships are sought and valued. This combination of types often possesses much charisma and others enjoy their company greatly. They are natural and gracious hosts or hostesses and love to throw parties and gather friends together for celebrations. They have great generosity of spirit and love to give of themselves for the betterment of others.

In times of stress, however, the 2W3, who perceives other's feelings so strongly, can be overwhelmed by the needs of others and even their own repressed emotions. Because types Two and Three both belong in the heart-centered triad, they lack the self-awareness that the influence of a head or body (such as One) type would lend to them. This particular marriage of types can lead to over-sensitivity if they are on the receiving end of criticism. Their sense of pride can become over-inflated, which might lead to authoritarian behaviour and outbursts of anger.

Advice for the Helper

Take care to look after your own self-care. You are so busy empathizing with other people and supporting them in their needs, that you forget your own needs in the process. Your own requirements are just as important as everybody else's. It is important to set and maintain your own personal boundaries and to ensure that you get adequate rest, exercise and proper nutrition. Do not change yourself in order to win approval from another. By being yourself and establishing boundaries, you can give to others more authentically, and you can only be of real service to others if you are balanced, healthy and centered within yourself.

Before you help somebody, consider whether or not they actually need or want your help in the first place. Have they asked for your assistance? Make sure that you are not just imposing your ideas of the way things should be upon them and interfering unnecessarily. Furthermore, it is not up to you to demand gratitude or decide the manner in which such gratitude is expressed. Instead, try asking people directly what it is they really need. Just because you can sense the need of another, does not necessarily mean that they would like you to step in and 'solve' all their problems for them. You must be willing to accept a "no, thank you" if that is what's forthcoming. This should not be taken as rejection.

In the event of you doing something nice for someone, there is no need whatsoever to remind them of it. This is a temptation you need to resist. It will only make the other party question your motivation for helping them in the first place and will cause them to be uncomfortable. They might also withdraw from you altogether, if you choose to behave in this way. Let kindness be its own reward!

Understand that people express their affection and appreciation in lots of different ways. Just because it is in a manner that is not instantly recognizable to you and not necessarily a way which you would have chosen yourself, does not mean that they do not care. Learn to recognize the different manifestations of love.

Make sure you are honest about your own motives and that you are not lying to yourself about why you are helping someone. If you are just doing it in order to receive gratitude, this is not a healthy motive and you might well be setting yourself up for disappointment. You must guard against co-dependency at all times.

Chapter 5: The Triads, The Heart And Soul Of The Enneagram

As mentioned in previous chapters, there is much more to the enneagram model than just the basic outline of it. There are many add-ons to the basic nine types under the enneagram, which allow for the results of any given test to be much more individually—it makes your results that much more meant for you and you alone.

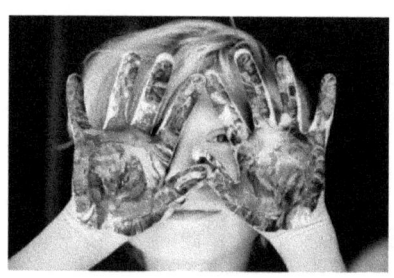

Along with the basic shape of the enneagram, we also have the centers and the wings of the diagram. There are three centers in the enneagram, which more broadly categorize the nine types into 3 categories by their center. Types eight, nine, and one are the instinctive centers, while two, three, and four have the feeling center and five, six, and seven are aligned within the thinking center. The center of your personality type can offer you more insight in particular into how you make judgements and decisions, and what will likely pose the largest threat to your mental health.

The instinctual center is, as the name suggests, the group of personality types which is most likely to act on gut instinct. This group is less likely to believe in spiritualistic ideals, like coincidence, karma, and a higher power. However, those within the instinctual center are often very loyal, and tend to be proficient at detecting a farce, or finding out a person which they sense may be lying or otherwise not who they say they are. As the title suggests of them, these types—

eight, nine, and one—are especially good at using their intuition, tapping into their "gut feeling" on things. However, this can sometimes mean that someone with an instinctual center won't be able to cut their losses, sometimes going farther than is necessary, believing that they gut instincts will never fail them. This can spell trouble for these types, and they may have trouble trusting real, reliable sources, if their intuition does not agree. The times where their intuition turn out to be wrong, however, are usually quite slim, and their gut feelings will serve them well, much more often than not. This headstrong type likes to act without thinking, and usually doesn't like to take the time to stop and contemplate what they've done or why they've done it. This can cause issue for them, especially when their gut instinct turns out to be wrong.

The feeling center is made up of the three types who are willing to do most anything to gain the emotional and psychological validation of themselves and others, especially figures that they look up to. This could mean a parental figure or a teacher, or a lifelong friend. Regardless, this figure in can become to fixation of the feeling center's life at times, as they may have trouble finding it in themselves to be happy and independently content. Often, the feeling center is prone to acting on a whim, doing bold things they wouldn't otherwise do when the feeling strikes them as right. They can clash with the thinking centers specifically, as the feeling types—two, three, and four—may take personal offense to something the thinking center said without considering their emotions. This vulnerability of the feeling types can harm them at times, but it also makes them an incredibly valuable asset. In a professional setting, someone who is able to tap into their feeling center and still control their emotions can be especially skilled at empathizing with an audience or a market. In the context of personal relationships, someone with a feeling center can be a blessing or a curse, depending on the day. On a good day, a feeling type is loving, empathetic, considerate, and cooperative. On bad days, however, the feeling types can become wrathful, petty, or vengeful. This proneness to attitude shifts and mood swings can badly damage the reputation of the feeling type, but when they can level their feelings and look at their surrounding with a clear mind, they're experts at connecting successfully to all kinds of people.

Finally, the thinking centers come off as the stereotype of a cold, standoffish, perhaps overly analytical addition to the group. In reality, this is likely someone who understands the harshness of the world sometimes. They know what it's like to experience slumps, just like everyone else. A thinking center isn't someone overly harsh or unwilling to open up to people, but these traits may be ones that the thinking center should watch out for. Thinking centers are more prone to depressive episodes and periods of their lives than other people, and they're also more prone to harsh slips of the tongue. Sometimes, thinking centers get so wrapped up in their own intensity that they don't realize that, to some other people, their passion comes off as harsh and cold. Tone is a tricky thing, especially with the thinking center. They aren't sure if what they're saying sounds correct, and they have trouble gauging the responses from those around them, which can leave them at a loss for a clear answer— something massively frustrating to a thinking center. Not being able to understand clearly how to solve a problem, and having to fumble through nuances and reading between the lines, can be hell for a thinking center. If someone with a thinking center can, however, learn to control their frustration, they can easily become a powerful force of logic. The analytic prowess of many thinking centers makes them indispensable, both in a professional group and a friend unit. The thinking center is much more likely to serve in a friend group as the voice of reason, keeping their companions in cheque and making sure that people think their way through decisions before they make them. Thus, they can clash with the raw emotions of many feeling centers, and they may take an instinctual center's disregard for logic as a personal attack on themselves. If the thinking center can get their never-ending thirst for understanding under control, there's no doubt that they become important allies, in any line of work and in all aspects of their lives.

Each of the three centers also have a singular emotion which is the dominant feeling for that center, when a person within that center loses control of themselves emotionally. When you get into an argument and leave from that argument with the issue unresolved, how are you most likely to feel?

If you think you would most likely still feel angry, hateful, or full of rage at the other person—regardless of whether or not someone is right or wrong, or if that person is you—you probably belong to one of the types within the instinctive center. Those in the feeling center are most likely to feel shame for their outbursts, while the thinking center may fear the consequences before they feel a moral weight or guilt.

Even within those three centers and their primary response to stressful scenarios, all types react to their main emotional theme differently from one another. A type one and a type eight aren't very similar, and yet they both experience anger as their primary negative response. However, a type one will often deal with their feelings of anger or rage by suppressing it as much as possible. They direct their negative feelings into a desire for control of themselves and others. A type eight will more simply act out immediately when they feel anger this way, the most likely to lash out—but also the least likely to harbor these feelings of anger for a very long time. Because all types and all people are inherently different, the enneagram is also shaped around these different responses, within both the types and within the center that those types are squared away in.

There are also the triads—these three triads present another way that groups of the nine basic types relate to the world and process it, each in a slightly different way. These groups of three are often called the "harmony triads"--they each give us three types within which react differently to their experiences. Again, the way that each of these triads relate to the world is not exclusive only to those types inside of them—all of these outlooks are also the result of experiences an individual has. It's up to you if you want to adopt an outlook like this or incorporate more traits of one or more of these triads into your life and relationships.

The first triad is made up of types three, six, and nine—these are the three base personalities which make up the pragmatic triad, also referred to be some as the "Earth triad" or the "attachment triad". These types are people who are more in control of the way we thrive in our material world. In particular, each of these types has, in a manner of speaking, removed themselves from something important in the ways of attachment, or for the sake of attachment. Type three is more likely to have strayed from hope—giving up on wishful thinking in order to pursue the material world, a world that they may think can't exist in the same realm as hope. Type six is more likely to have strayed from faith—they're prone to the "life isn't fair" mentality, and are therefore more prone to resign from hope that their "luck" will turn around. Type nine, on the other hand, is more likely to have given up on the concept of quality love—specifically, type nine is prone to prioritizing the love and care for self below the cares and needs of others. This can lead to declining mental health in a type nine, as they may not see the importance of caring for themselves. Not likely to have their heads stuck in the clouds, the pragmatic triad is much more prone to seeking our straight-forward answers to what may seem like complex questions, often being comfortable settling for a secure place in the world. Often the ones to first utilize Occam's razor—the principle which states that the answer to a problem which is the most simple and straightforward is often the correct one—the down-to-earth group are the ones who connect us at our deepest and simplest level, and the ones who are more likely to communicate more physically than put their feelings into words. This can also mean they're prone to acting before they thoroughly consider all their options, which can easily place them in hot water. Pragmatists may seem cold and distant, much like the thinking center, but they are people who want to be cared for and looked after just as much as anyone else, although they may have trouble realizing this at first. If someone can get through to them and convince them that there's nothing wrong with wanting help, they can be in a much better place mentally.

The second triad of the enneagram is made up of types two, five, and eight. They are also known as the relationist triad, the types which show us how we should offer things to others in order to sustain relationships. They care for others and a lot of the identity of these types revolves around what they can and will do for those around them, whether they be someone that person is deeply involved with, or just a work acquaintance. Specifically, type two is more adept at offering care and support, as the friend who may not jump to offer you a solution to your problem, but who will listen quietly and empathize. Type five is more likely to distance themselves from the problem at hand in order to get a new and rational perspective on it. Less likely to empathize as much, but much more likely to offer you a rational solution to your problem which is more likely to solve the issue or prevent it from happening. Type eight, on the other hand, is more likely to shield you from the issue at hand, even if they can't offer you a surefire solution to it. While the second type offers empathy and vulnerability, the eights type offers strength and protection in whatever way they can. It's in this manner that all of the relationist types find their way to help and serve others in any way they can, although this can sometimes mean they prioritize the needs of those around them above the needs and desires of their own. If the relationists can really solidify a way to care for themselves before catering to the wants of others, then they can be much happier in their lives. Although relationists may seem as though they want to shield others, they're a bit different from the empathetic feeling center—the relationist triad very much wants to be shielded just as much as they shield others. However, they have trouble communicating this to the people who they help out, as they don't want to intrude or make them feel lesser.

Types one, four, and seven make up the third triad of the enneagram, often referred to as the utopists or the idealists of the enneagram, are the kinds of people who try to find ways in which the world could be improved upon, how we could change ourselves and others around us for the better so that the world as a whole would be made into a better place. This triad is also often called the "frustration" triad, as their vision for the idealist future is always clouded over by the reality of the world, especially by their personal situation. This can leave them disillusioned with the world—frustrated by their own ideals and how impossible they often seem—and by themselves—frustrated that their ideals are so unreachable, or frustrated that they can't seem to find the time, resources, or energy to make their utopia into reality. Specifically, the first type seeks more of an idealist world according to their own standard of what a utopia is. This can, unfortunately, make the first enneagram type seem self-centered, as they may not necessarily view the ideals of others as equal to their own. Type four seeks out a utopia, a world where everyone's needs and wants are catered to materially. Thus, they're incredibly frustrated at times when this standard is very rarely met in the "real" world. Finally, type seven is the most hedonistic of this triad, as their utopia is shaped around the prioritization of good emotions and experienced. Their ideal world is often one in which everyone is happy at all times. However, they're frustrated when people experience bad things in the world. Similar to a child's empathy for all things living and nonliving, the seventh type's heart goes out to everyone in the world who experiences pain or suffering, no matter to what degree or what type—themselves included. This triad is the one who seeks to better the way we live our lives, but is often shackled by how far ahead they tend to plan. This triad may be the individuals on a team who has a fantastic end goal, but has no idea how to execute the plan at all. When cooperating, all three of the triads make up an idea team—if the idealist can settle for an optimistic but attainable dream, the relationist can reign in their need to help others while still managing themselves and their own empathy, and the pragmatist can learn to understand all different kinds of perspectives, then all three can work together and form the ideal plan or end result.

All of these centers and triads are additional information that you'll receive at the end of the enneagram test, but they only contextualize onto the pre-existing result of the test. The center and the triad in which you belong only categorize you further. The wings, on the other hand, add on to the basic nine of the enneagram types. In your results for the enneagram test, you will find which of the nine types you more closely represent, but you will also gain more insight into your wing. Your wing is a kind of second aspect of your personality, the background of your main type which adds context and other important features to you and your behavior as a whole. This means that two people who are both a type nine may be entirely different, with one of them having an eight-wing and the other possessing a one-wing. The wing type which connects itself to your basic type will always be one of the types which is adjacent to your basic type; a type three can have a two-wing or a four-wing, but not a wing type of any of the other six personalities.

There's actually a major disagreement between many experts of the enneagram as to whether or not any given person can only have one wing on top of their base personality, or whether it's possible to have two wings instead.

Most all people agree that even if a person has two wings on top of their base personality type, everyone will always have a more dominant of the two wings. Having two wings that are equally influential to a person's behavior could be detrimental, as it opens the possibility for many more direct discrepancies in personality traits and behavioral patterns in the different types that someone identifies with. So, in any test that you may take on the enneagram, including the one within this book, there will only be one "wing" addressed—although two supposedly coexist, the dominant one is so much more relevant to your results that to mention the other "non-dominant" wing would be verbose.

Some people speculate that, as they grow older, their "second wing" becomes more prominent in them, and begins to actually contribute much to themselves in the way of their personality. Whether or not this development is contributed solely to the physical and psychological maturing process, or it turns out to be an actual process that is independent of our personalities natural shifts and changes remains to be seen. Still, the developing of your personality is shown to change and grow as you yourself grow, which again lends itself to the reuse of the enneagram test more than once over the course of your life, to receive a greater and more contextual understanding of yourself and your relations.

So, how do the centers and the wings of your enneagram play into your overall results, and what those results translate to in your life? As we learn and grow, as do our personalities. It's not that one experience is replaced by another if the lesson if those experiences contradict each other. Rather, you learn from two contradictory experiences that one answer, one side of a coin, is not always the only correct one. You learn to consider multiple angles of all situations, or at least learn the importance of doing so. The same goes for your enneagram. While, yes, the arguably most important part of your results in your base type, the center in which you fall and the wing—or wings—which connect you to that basic type also play a massive role when considering your personality, especially how your personality changes over time. As you grow and learn, both your base enneagram type and your center and wings will become more important to that development. Again, the enneagram is not a step-by-step guide on how to live your life as you grow older, but it is a guide that helps you make sense of the world around you, and can help you grow and learn on your own.

Chapter 6: The Japanese Restaurant Story

Self-esteem and self-confidence determine personal and professional fulfillment. It is the key to accessing your goals. The lack of self-confidence translates into a devaluation of the person: phrases like "I am worthless", "I am not able", "I have no quality" are on the agenda in the inner dictionary of those who lack self-esteem. Those who lack confidence in themselves often struggle to draw up a list of their qualities.

Being aware of your qualities is essential to encourage and nurture self-esteem, but to grow and improve as people and professionals, you need to be aware of your areas of development. You have to question yourself and work on what you can improve: your flaws.

Here is another important exercise for you: take a sheet and write a list of your defects.

This exercise will probably be easier than the previous one. Once you have compiled the list of defects, take one and decide to improve it. Daily constancy and frequency are important. Do you always have negative thoughts? Try for 30 days to replace negative thoughts with positive messages. If it is not enough 30 days extended until the target is reached and go to the next defect. If you really commit yourself, you can get rid of 6 defects in a year. The aim is not to achieve perfection, but to improve and increase your personal value.

Remember that being aware of your defects also means knowing how to accept them and avoid putting yourself in difficult situations.

Now I want to ask you something: can you say thank you?

Say it three times in a loud voice.

Learn to accept compliments, don't refuse them, but answer THANK YOU. If the feedback does not come spontaneously then ask for it "how did I feel during my conference speech?", "I was effective?" If you answer negatively you will know what to improve, if you receive a compliment it will be sugar for your self-esteem.

Maybe not everyone knows it but learning to compliment is really essential to have a greater self-awareness because it allows you to have a better relationship with compliments, whatever they are. In fact the first step to receive them is to make them.

Making compliments means being attentive to people, observing them and this is very pleasing.

Now I tell you what you will do to improve this aspect of yourself, during this week in a sincere and authentic way you make a compliment following a good deed that you intend to reinforce.

At first it may seem like a stretch, but as you compliment it it will come naturally to you and you will become a distributor of natural smiles.

I just have to ask you to have the maximum honesty in this exercise, you have to always and only tell the truth and don't give compliments if they are not sincere and authentic because in this case the lies would have the exact opposite effect and they would distance you from your final resolution goal and awareness of your inner person.

I want to tell you a story. And it's a story that really happened when I was twenty-four and I lived in Seattle. I had just graduated and was looking for a job. I was a smart boy, I had few good friends but in college I was one of those who studied diligently but never exaggerated. I liked going out with friends but I didn't particularly love parties. We went to eat a pizza and watch a movie at the cinema, sometimes I took a girl out for a date. I was a quiet boy with a normal life. I had my ambitions, but they were still submerged by life and youth. One day I was with two friends of mine in a new downtown Japanese restaurant. It was a very elegant place, with precious antique vases in the hall, wonderful prints on the wall and an atmosphere that exuded opulence. Before that I had been eating sushi in some place near the college, but no place was like that. When I crossed the threshold of that Japanese restaurant I felt with a one-way ticket for the inconvenience, I was entering a place that I wasn't completely familiar with and where I was finding too many details of unease. The waiters were dressed in elegant suits and spoke slowly with a fake smile on their faces. They looked at me and watched my clothing. Maybe they thought I was too young for a place like that. Maybe they thought my jeans and my unbranded shirt were not the most appropriate attire for their restaurant. It was called "Empire of the Sun: Japanese Restaurant". The name already expressed the whole concept of those precious vases and those prints on the wall. My friend

Tom had come to my house that afternoon and asked me if I wanted to go and try that new restaurant, I said yes without enthusiasm I didn't like changing habits and for me the Japanese restaurant was only one until then. His name was Yoshi and was frequented by all the college kids. We liked it because it was cheap and Seattle's prettiest girls went there too. And then after dinner the waiter came and offered you a small bottle of cold sake to digest. It was perfect. But that night we weren't there, my friends and I were in this new restaurant and I was going to figure out one of the greatest lessons of my life.

My friends and I looked at each other for a moment, then we all looked at the waiter and overcoming the sense of annoyance and discomfort we all felt we entered and followed him to our table. We had arrived there and none of us would have ever had the courage to say "let's go this place is not for us". We sat down, we looked at each other with a hesitant look but now we were there. The table was elegantly set with precious ceramic bowls. A waitress gives me the menu, I take it and open it. The various dishes were written in Japanese and the prices were exorbitant. That dinner would have cost me half of what I had on my bank account. I was sure every dish would be delicious, but I was not such a keen Japanese cooking enthusiast that I wanted to spend all that money on a dinner. I could not. I was young and I had a precarious job, I still had to realize myself. I don't call myself a stingy person, but I am a man who has always valued money. This is my being. This is my way of life. It's part of me. I felt the weight of what was happening on my shoulders and I absolutely didn't want to be at that moment. But what could I do? Here then is that at that moment my head, my mind made a mental click. There was a real leap. I realized that I absolutely must not deny myself and my way of seeing the world. I must always give priority to my feeling. Always. So I looked at my friends and simply told them what I thought, we left. Probably the waiter thought we were poor, but the moral of this whole story is that I don't care at all about what other people think. Or rather, I care because I am not a self-centered person who thinks only of himself but I understand that the decisions I make must be decisions that make me feel good and that do not obscure everything that I am. And this happens both in big decisions like buying a house or changing jobs, and in smaller decisions like deciding to get up from the table because menu prices are too expensive. This is great advice, I give you this rule of life, never underestimate its importance.

When you want to get up from the table, any table, do it and follow your instincts.

I just named the word instinct. What does it mean?

We often name it but it is not always clear what it really means. Acting by instinct, seeking a flow of actions without being held back by the structures that a person can build when he thinks too much and does not follow his own desires.

The word instinct indicates an action or behavior performed by an animal or a person automatically, without being aware of it, due to an internal force within the organism.

The definition of instinct, in this sense, also extends to purely psychic and mental actions, such as, for example, the same cognitive activity, which can be considered as a natural instinct, unlike those psychic processes that are based on patterns I learned.

According to the psychology of common sense, animal behavior is essentially based on instincts, which allow the survival of individual animals and their species through the satisfaction of the primary needs of hunger, thirst, sleep and sex.

Human behavior, on the other hand, would be only minimally instinctive, because even actions aimed at satisfying primary needs would be guided by conscience and shaped by social and cultural factors.

The theme of instinct is strongly connected with the practice of the Enneagram and it is not possible to understand the whole structure of this ancient knowledge without understanding in depth the theme of instinct and the various types of first-born strength that push us to commit a certain action . When a person does not know this subject and studies only the "nine types" he inevitably makes important mistakes in identifying his own personality or the personality of other people, thus unjustly attributing characteristics to the nine profiles and running the risk of stereotyping. But there is another even more relevant reason: only those who explore the theme of instincts are able to open an important front of inner work, with themes that are responsible for some of the most rooted and "neurotic" aspects of our personalities.

Instincts concern survival strategies that all animals (even animals that are not mammals) adopt, in different areas. Although there are different types of instincts - such as maternal, masculine or feminine, for example - in the Enneagram we study three specific types of instincts: the conservative (also known as self-conservative), the social and the sexual. All these instincts belong to what is conventionally called the instinctive center in the contemporary movement of the Enneagram, linked to the most visceral, automatic, rapid and unconscious sensations and reactions we have; reactions that are mainly commanded by our primitive brain, also called reptilian brain.

Some things are non-negotiable, that is, they must happen. Thus, the behaviors deriving from the instinctive field are part of our level of being, that "animal soul" which comes to dominate in some situations or which remains latent in others. The important thing is therefore to be able to arrive at a more opportune possibility of equilibrium. These behaviors come from a level of being lower than the human level and still much more distant from the level of being more directly linked to Essence, which is the most evolved part of each of us. Instincts are related to a part of us that is inferior to our personality and that can be called a false personality.

If our personality, as shown by the Enneagram through the lower emotional and mental center, shows us our passions and fixations, we must understand that this is already a great distortion of what we really are, instincts are still a level distortion inferior that they form a mask on our existence, and therefore represent a distortion of our own personality.

When the functioning of instincts is healthy, instincts come into action in a manner pertinent to a given situation and always to the right extent. In this case the instincts do not take care of such a significant part of our life experience and leave room for the most refined centers of intelligence.

In the healthy use of one's instincts, for example, the self-conservative instinct is the one that fortunately comes into action to protect us when our physical survival begins to be truly threatened - for example in times of financial crisis, when we are hungry or sleepy , during a very cold climate, or during a robbery.

To increase confidence in yourself, you have to get out of the established patterns, with reassuring habits. Pay attention to everything you do every day because the principle to remember is one step at a time, gently, without revolutions.

Make a list of small challenges! From the most "easy" to the most "difficult" for you.

Start with the first challenge. Until it is won, don't go to the next one!

No pressure, if it takes you two months it's not serious. The goal is simply to move, change habits.

The social instinct is the one that comes into action to help us produce, among other things, the very important experiences of belonging, of collaborating and connecting - and in healthy use it tends to come into action only at times when these things are more at risk or when they are desirable.

The sexual instinct, on the other hand, is activated to allow us to create closer ties with other individuals, by means of a true union and communion, through the experiences of connection with vital energy, like the whole - and, once again, it tends to go into action only when these constraints begin to falter or when they have to increase a little.

Instincts also hide both deeper shadows and characteristics related to spiritual functions and the higher nature of the human being. They also hide, in my opinion, some secrets of what I call our soul schema, and of specific spiritual lineages. In the following articles I will briefly discuss some of these aspects.

However, unfortunately, the general state of the human being is very limited due to a much diminished conscience. Therefore, the vast majority of people experience strong distortions in the use of instincts, due to unresolved traumas and complexes, which, unconsciously, make us lose the due energy balance in relation to instincts. Instincts become more active and begin to command our daily experience of living, so as to overlap with our emotions and our thoughts, greatly limiting the quality of our existence. More specifically, each instinct distorts so as to operate above or below the appropriate level, all those times we perceive a feeling of threat in that specific sphere of life. All this usually happens at a profoundly unconscious level, but it must be unmasked by people engaged with their own self-development.

In summary there are two ways in which these distortions arrive:

The first mode occurs when we experience (usually unreal) threats to the sphere of life corresponding to a specific instinct and, as a reaction, we make sure that this instinct functions above its normal and desirable level, that is, when we unconsciously pass to the attempt to compensate for that feeling of scarcity or risk with a level in excess of that instinctive function.

The second mode occurs when the threats we perceive (these too usually unreal), linked to a specific instinct, ensure that an opposite strategy is developed: that of reducing the level of functioning of that instinctive energy, which will then become insufficient and underused.

The third instinct tends to be more balanced, or to have some of the first or second strategy. Therefore it is the only one that tends to use closer to reality.

Depending on the specific distortion made by the person, behaviors, profiles and potentially very different problems arise between them. This happens at such a point that we can say that every order of instinct carries typical traces of people. In other words, the order of instincts generates a second typology within the Enneagram system, parallel to the most known typology, that of the Nine Types. Indeed, individuals with the same dominant and repressed instinct can often feel more similar to each other than individuals of the same enneatype who have different instinctive profiles. In the subject of relationships, for example, the instinctive profile is more relevant than the classic one, of the nine Enneagrams. And if sometimes the instinctive profile of an individual can be added to the profile of its enneatype, in some cases it can even contrast with some typical features expected.

Chapter 7: Why Choose Enneagram And What Are The Benefits You Can Get From It?

Either consciously or unconsciously, we must have shown or exuded a particular character that must have put us within a circle of those nine personalities. These nine personalities help us shape our lives for the better, as they allow us to alter and improve our interactions with the world. The knowledge we acquire through Enneagram helps us to understand with more experience about what the world is all about. Additionally, it helps us understand our emotional reactions and how to defend our behavior, the behavior of others, our highest qualities, and our purpose in life.

The new world order focuses on the interaction between us. Thanks to globalization, we can no longer stay in a state of autarky even if we really want to. Enneagram allows us to focus our energy into making sure these interactions between ourselves are fostered and improved in every way. Instead of being dependent on our emotions and following the dictates of these many emotions that we tend to feel in regard to our relationships with others. Enneagram would give us the power to stay aware and in control of these emotions and in turn, understand the personality of any individuals we are interacting with. That way, we would achieve success, motivation, and attention in the long run.

Ask yourself, are you finding it extremely difficult to have a long-term relationship? Are your connections with your friends and families strained as a result of misconception or an emotional breakdown? Are you finding it difficult to understand and relate with the people around you, either at home or your workplace? If so, then this chapter is for you. Immerse yourself in it and make sure you digest every word to the best of your abilities.

There are different benefits to Enneagram, but here we will only focus on some of the more prominent ones. The Enneagram or the study of personality can help you on a personal level and in your relationships too. It can also help people in their professions and businesses.

Also, the Enneagram equips us with the appropriate tools to bring about profound change within ourselves so that we can bring a balance to our lives. It helps us keep clear thoughts and straight heads so that we can conquer the problems of our lives instead of being consumed by them. The benefits stated here are based on the general usage and understanding of Enneagram. They include:

- Adequate awareness of people's personalities in the world no matter how unconventional:

Beyond your experience in life, Enneagram makes you aware of how people could behave. For example, in an unfamiliar community, the knowledge of enneagram personalities help to create an awareness of the possible behavior patterns you may encounter. That way, you will be able to see beyond your own limited experiences and perceptions. In other words, knowing other people's personality as well as yours makes relating to people more comfortable. With this awareness, it is easier to live our lives fully and also maintain a healthier relationship.

- Successful relationships in all ramifications:

Using Enneagram would undoubtedly make sure that the relationships that you keep both at work and at home are a success. This is true because by understanding our own unconscious reactions to situations, we can be more understanding and flexible when dealing with other people's responses to similar situations. Thus, allowing us to see it as normal for people to react to actions. We would equally develop a well-prepared mind and compassion to whatever their behavior turns out to be.

- Enhancing tolerance

With the knowledge of Enneagram, you are able to be aware of what people will likely say. Thus you take things less personally. When you know your personality type, it is easier to relate, and when there is a problem, you will be able to handle it with caution knowing full well that you could have handled it the same way or worse. The negative feeling you get when people treat you negatively would have less of an impact on you and become less painful to you. This is because you are now aware of their personalities. Your tolerance is heightened because you understand the decision-making processes of various kinds of personalities.

- Rapid personal growth:

Being able to identify the different types of personalities through Enneagram involves taking an in-depth look at the emotion, and the psychology of them, as well as how they allow us to grow beyond measures. After all, self-awareness leads to personal development and empathy in the judgment of others. When you possess the ability to develop your mental and emotional strength because you have a complete understanding of your personality and development, you are able to handle the challenges that come from dealing with people a lot better. Many positive changes can be expected as the ability to harness your personality traits develops and grows. In general, intellectual development is achieved during the process of coming to terms with one's personality and managing its accompanying challenges.

- Improvement of positive thinking

It doesn't matter who you are, once you understand the Enneagram personalities and their traits your mindset will change. You will experience a change in how negative reactions that you encounter impact your relationships because you're already aware of and familiar with their personality. You will live with less doubt and skepticism because you are more informed about actions and reactions. And, you will be at peace with everyone around because they are more comfortable with you based on the fact that you understand them.

- Adequate management of challenging relationships:

There are always situations where people of different minds come together to share ideas. With an understanding of Enneagram, you will be able to manage anyone's feelings about any situation that arises. Once you identify your personality type, and you know the strengths and weaknesses you possess, you will be able to interact with people of different personality types more effectively and healthily. The way they view things might be different from yours but with correct handling and management, opposing and challenging people of varying personality types can be successfully managed. You will build an immune system that helps you manage opposing behaviors from your colleagues at work because of the understanding of Enneagram personalities.

•Helps with parenting

While parenting can be an incredibly difficult task, with the knowledge of Enneagram, parents are able to demystify children's personalities and improve understanding. The way in which children change as they grow and develop can be better understood, allowing the parent/child relationship to strengthen when it often becomes more challenging. This is because children have the ability to exhibit multiple personality types within the same year. Not only that, but parent's personalities can differ from their children's greatly. However, understanding the Enneagram makes it easier for parents to know how to relate with them. This is why parents have found Enneagram very interesting –much of what it is about will be discussed later in this book.

•Enhancing recognition of both emotional and physical needs

Through the study of the Enneagram, everyone is aware of the need to maintain healthy, physical, and emotional needs plus care. People will take more care not to be a source of emotional unbalance. With the understanding of who you are and your flaws, you will be able to understand what you need at any given time. People of shy personalities or the personality type of Investigators -who love confinement-, will know how to manage their behaviors. They will know when to be confined and when to mix and relate with others. Enneagram personalities would keep affected and educated people abreast with the fact that emotions are one of the primary things that make up a person.

- Ability to avoid dispute

With the help of mutual understanding of enneagram personalities, conflict rates are reduced significantly among people. This is not because these series of misunderstandings won't occur. As a matter of fact, they will definitely come through no matter how little some of them are. However, the fact that there is background knowledge of what the personalities involved are would undoubtedly make these misunderstandings easier to manage and deal with.

The understanding of Enneagram could be more beneficial to people within the same business patterns. More so, gatherings, where opinions are solicited, would find Enneagram very relevant and helpful. The nature of the conflict is a bridge in normalcy and abnormality of things. Thus, solving and finding common ground as regards this conflict would see to the success and development of a relationship. That said, if people can have the same perception of things, there is a great tendency, they react in the same way.

Well there you have it, a few of the outstanding benefits you stand to gain from the Enneagram. Believe it or not, your life would be far better with Enneagram in it. When you practice this particular concept in your life, you are bound to enjoy blissfulness and blessedness. So what are you waiting for?

In conclusion, the reasons and benefits of Enneagram are felt most when you understand the context of its usage. Enneagram understanding creates a wide range of peace and harmonious co-existence in all ramifications, especially in the life of those working side-by-side with one another. Take advantage of the knowledge of Enneagram, and improve your life!

Chapter 8: Subtypes In Enneagram

Intuitive comprehension

Enneagram subtype - an introduction

By Peter O'Hara

The two Anagrams describe the three centers of intelligence: our mental center, where we have our thoughts, plans, and language; Our emotional center, where we have our feelings and our sympathy for other people; And the body center, where we have three important spontaneous drives. These are called self-preservation, social and one to one (or sexual) instinct. We use these three instincts for the things of each day's life. However, one of these instincts is more important to us and affects how we classify our character types. This main instinct interacts in our Enneagram way to create a "subtype". So for every 9 Enneagram types, there are three required subtype variations. Our path in life is formed through each personality type and subtype.

Three instinct

Two intuitive centers are based on our bodies. A major phase of work with this center is actually to be "in our body," a whole flow of life force that moves with us. There are different possibilities here as well - the ability to revel in physical pleasure and sensation, to keep our fitness and vitality, to travel as the natural world and wonderful traps of life itself. But much bigger than this. According to Ingram, we have three precise smooth drives:

The Self Renewal Instinct fabric controls our desires for resources and security, such as food, shelter, warmth, and domestic relationships.

One to one intuition controls our sexuality, our intimate relationships and close friendships, and the vitality of the life force within our bodies.

Social instincts govern our needs and membership within the larger group and community.

Intuitive comprehension

There are 27 subtypes for each of the 27 person types - the three versions - depending on which of our three trends.

Our subtypes describe our pioneering concerns and focus of attention to everyday existence - human beings and actions that are most important to us.

The sub-type pastime is, in part, a way to discharge or unheard of our character-type obsession or "low emotional habit".

Subtype patterns and habits are one of the major ways that we "fall asleep" in each day's life.

Each subtype has a different innate ability and is practical to excel in a specific area of spontaneous life.

How to find out your subtype

Two For some, their major subtype appears very clear, while for others it is a memory of study and exploration over time. Those who understand us properly may also have some beneficial feedback because we are no longer able to consistently see ourselves purposefully. This can be a bit tricky due to the fact that we have all three instincts at work in our lives. So you too can experience with all three intuitive names for your Enneagram type. But which of these three areas is necessary overall?

Considering the list of nine names for each subtype. In different words, do not appear only on the names for your Enneagram point, but instead on each of the three lists. One of these sets of 9 words will likely be more familiar to you than the two separately. If you had to choose between them, which spontaneous title would describe your group's concerns, habits, and prejudice over a long run - 9 self-maintenance words, 9 social words, or nine one-to-one words? (With a diagram of three "intuitive", think on each of these and select the set that speaks to you the most).

The set of two two two two nine phrases that you experience the most reflects your fundamental tendency, and consequently your particular subtype. Our attention to the route regularly shifts backward from one spontaneous place to another. We can also spend weeks or months in one intuition field and then move to another, relying on our opportunities or interests. But in the larger photo of our lives, one of these domains will be more of a concern, or more compelling to us than the others.

Do two two two two 2 are titles are incredibly inefficient. They are meant to arouse or anticipate a certain subject. If you don't find a subtype with a name on your talk, look at the names of the two factors to see if they fit.

SELF PRESERVATION SUBTYPES

Point One - Anxiety (Pioneer)

This subtype can be both very anxious or very self-controlled. Achievements of clothing as a way of being an accurate person about survival and safety and doing the proper work are included. It seems necessary to subdue nature and impose order on the natural world. Families, households, food preparation, etc. take precedence over various needs. However, too much self-sacrifice can gasp physical anxiety and resentment.

Point Two - Privilege

This subtype excels in developing warm, personal relationships with many people. Because of this incredible ability and amount of interest spent in helping and nurturing others, it can be a feeling when it comes to fulfilling a person's personal desires, or "me first,". This may additionally contribute to an arrogant attitude. Or the insistence on going last helps another type of specialty, such as in false ways.

Point Three - Security (Company man or woman)

With this subtype, the ability of the three to work hard, work well and have perfect photos is placed in the carrier of physical success. With their significant pressure and energy, this sub-type can fulfill their desires for monetary security, a luxurious home, etc. The risk in this endeavor is losing contact with one's real self and becoming highly recognized with one's role at work.

Four points - fearlessness (creative individualist)

This is to jump, pack and move in new situations, get up or take risks when the risk instinct is highlighted, or when the appropriate lifestyle looks elsewhere. To others, it may also appear carefree, such as throwing winds carefully, though it may work properly with an unconventional, creative or artistic style. There is a concern here between trying to raise physical security and feeling isolated from it all.

Five Points - Home (Castle Defender)

Do two houses are a fort and an area far from the world and safe. There is concern about having enough material that can lead to hoarding. On the other hand, this subtype may additionally disappear in allegiance to any geographic location, always moving or moving to the surrounding area with a domestic in a backpack or tourist van.

Six Point - Summer (Family Loyalists)

The style for this subtype is to remove fear by making connections and agreements with humans through the use of personal warmth. They choose not to live outside in the cold. Experiencing heat loss or a threat to their safety in lifestyles can cause risk-taking anxiety and need to stay within well-recognized boundaries.

Point Seven - Family (Gourmand)

Does Do Do This sub-type like to experience a quiet lifestyle within their home and in the circle of friends? The emphasis is on sharing appropriate ideas and conversations, getting ready hard material (or eating out), planning enjoyable projects. There may be problems with over talking, overeating and overstimulation.

Point Eight - Satisfactory Survival (Survivalist)

aggression and excess are added to physical survival and physical security. In an opposing world, they will win (or go down fighting). Strongly protecting friends and family, they can establish more territory and reserves than anyone. But in a favorable world, they may miss the boat entirely.

Point Nine - Hunger (Collector)

This sub-type enhances realistic infrastructure and day-to-day growing rhythms that support spontaneous living. But there is a tendency to "go to sleep" or intoxicate oneself, not only with food but with the consumption of all kinds of clothes. (They often hoard many items). Fabric abundance and a lifestyle of comfort can set off efforts towards personal or spiritual development.

Social issues

Adaptability in one point (social reformer)

This subtype is comfortable with a tightly closed social work and a clear set of rules. On their own grounds, they are generally quite pleasant and lavish. But their emphasis on doing things the right way can make it difficult to adapt to new situations, and can also cause resentment or criticism towards others who may additionally perform "incorrectly".

Point Two - Ambition (Ambassador)

The two self-esteem is earned through social approval and visible achievements. The empathy of two people and the ability to satisfy other people's desires are used to create an important, even important position within the agency or cause. Associating with the right man is generally more important than taking the center stage.

Point Three - Reputation (Politician)

power for success is directed towards winning social approval, understanding the appropriate people, and gaining strength in social institutions, whether it is in government, business, or community groups. True social management or sincere self-acclamation can occur through publicity and photo-making.

Four points - shame / respect (serious commentator)

feelings of scarcity can be aroused through social situations, directed jealousy to different people's fame or membership. This sub-type attempts to establish an appropriate social role for the group as emotional truth-tellers. Men or women want to get to the bottom of anxiety between seeking authenticity and social expectations. two

Five points - totem/symbol (professor)

in this subtype know about the sacred symbols of the team or society (Kuladevata) and knowledge of the language. Nevertheless, a greater emphasis on evaluation and interpretation can get in the way of participation and entice someone into the role of supervisor or learned teacher.

Point Six - Duty (Social Guardian)

It is worrying to be clear about one's role in a group or society. Knowing the guidelines and growing clear agreements with friends and colleagues are important for overcoming anxiety and eliminating rejection. Yet there may additionally be ambivalence about belonging. Carrying one's responsibility can be a call and burden for everyone.

Point Seven - Limit / Sacrifice (Utopian Visionary)

is a paradox here: social workers need the initiative of their friends and their crew to fulfill both their social idealism and love of life, but for the increasing suitability of the team or community itself Exploitation always involves some sacrifice. Individual expansion and planning have limitations for future outcomes.

Point Eight - Friendship / Social Reasons (Group Leader / Gang Leader)

This fashion is generally about overcoming powerlessness and injustice by being part of a coalition group in a management group. Anger and aggression are each mediated by using the wishes of the crew and used for the common agenda. Loyalty to people and social reason takes precedence over personal feelings and needs.

Point Nine - Partnership (Community Beneficiary)

This subtype blends properly with the fashion and agendas of their friends and a range of social groups. The excessive aspect is a selfless contribution to management and persistent good; Trouble is the tendency to "fall asleep" in a restful social position or of indiscriminate sleeping activities.

One person

Point One - Jealousy / Rapture (Evangelist)

Two two two two two two A relatively charged innate tendency is defended under strong will power with clear rules and requirements for right behavior, leading to more time than enthusiasm in everything. It is best to keep away from self-recruitment to take care of the partner. Jealousy towards a partner is common, and may additionally be experienced towards **individual humans who find more room for self-expression.**

Point Two - Temptation / Aggression (Lover)

Two two two two two for mutual connection and empathy is accessible to create the possible relationship of all and to win the acceptance of chosen human beings in a one-to-one relationship, even a brief one. The use of metaphorical language and feeling tones can be as efficient as seductive, though no longer always in the sexual sense. Or the same ability can be used in a more aggressive style that demands non-public interest and recognition.

Three points – femininitymasculinity (movie star)

Do two two two two The ability to create a successful picture focuses on gender identity and issues. Personal energy or charisma rests on eye-catching as a woman or a man. Nevertheless, there can be confusion about one's actual sexuality. There is a tendency to persist in a performance role, whether on display screen and stage or in personal relationships.

Four Point - Competition (Theatrical Person)

Two two two two two two competition with others is used to overcome the feeling of internal lack and create inspiration for non-public agendas. The energy or power of other people is taken as a non-public challenge and usually creates a strong response. One person's personal fees rise and fall compared to others.

Point Five - Privacy (Secret Agent)

Two two two two two two This is a sharing of the internal, personal world beliefs in one to one relationships. Personal relationships are carefully chosen. There may be a latent quality, or a kind of deep storehouse, that reflects some tension between the desire to make contact and the need to maintain autonomy.

Point Six - Strength or Beauty (Warrior)

Do two two two two two first fashion is mainly based on overcoming or worrying about the strength of the mind and the might of physical strength and valor, or through the power of one's mind and fierce ideological positions.

Do two two two two The fear and self-doubt of 2D fashion is perceived through eagerness for one's idealism and increasing grandeur in one's environment. This helps to create some stability and control.

Point intake - suggestion / feasibility (adventurer)

Two, two, two suggestions work both ways. One-to-one Sevens can easily be influenced through new ideas, adventures, and the attraction of people who fall into a country of alluring or "disillusionment". They also have fantastic powers of suggestion and can use personal appeals to lead people to a new paradigm, a new purchase, or a new relationship.

Point Eight - Possession / Surrender (Commander)

one-to-one eight use their strong and own emphasis (or control) to their partner or other people. They may additionally be said to be near this drive, which may not be favorable at times. The different side of it will display as a longing to meet so that someone can surrender and take it under control so that he can replace her as a partner.

Point nine - union (seeker)

One to one Nine is longing to merge the two with one partner, Prakriti or God. It may be indiscriminate or asymmetrical at times, but it may additionally be a gateway into a parodic position. In day-to-day lifestyles, it can show as a hassle with maintaining personal boundaries and attention, given that it is very convenient to be drawn outside of oneself.

A short questionnaire on instinct

SELF PRESERVATION

How important is your home? How much time and money do you spend at your home? Can you cross a new living space without difficulty?

How important is your family? Do you experience summer relationships with household members?

What is your current relationship to food - buying, preparing, eating? Do you like sharing your content with different people?

How much time and electricity do you spend on your physical health? Are you up to date in your fitness care appointments with doctors, dentists, etc.?

Do you feel financially secure? How much effort do you make to manage income and cash? Are you afraid of this? Is that enough one better than the other

How important is having an intimate relationship for you? If you are married, how much attention do you give to your partner?

Do you decide to spend time with your colleagues or close people one by one, or will you spend time with humans in a group?

What is the role of sexuality in your life?

Do you have a spiritual practice, or is there an area in your lifestyle that you transcend your everyday personality?

Chapter 9: Type Three - The Performer

Dominant Traits
- **Image-conscious**
- **Excellent**
- **Driven**
- **Adaptable**

General Behavior

Performers are results-driven. They are the type of personality that many supervisors and employers want in their teams. A performer is someone who is out for success; they almost lust for it. They will do the extraordinary to get results, and everyone who has them in their team knows it. If the team is stuck, this is one person you can call on to find a way through.

One of the defining characteristics of performers is their need for advancement. They never settle. In their lives, there is always something better to be found, so they are the last person you will expect to rest in a comfort zone. They chase after success because they believe they can be the best if they put their minds to it.

People love to relate with performers because of the inspiration in their lives. If you know one closely, you probably know the story of their success, because you have witnessed it. You know how hard they work, their commitment, their drive, and how passionate they are about what they do. Who wouldn't want to be associated with such a person?

A performer is someone who makes you think twice about the decisions you make. Interacting with them can make you change your ways because you have seen their great success, and you would gladly change your ways to enjoy something similar. It is no secret that they are role models for a lot of people.

Today a lot of people are living faux lives. Many portray themselves as successful when, in reality, they are just pretending. This lack of authenticity makes them shudder at the thought of being exposed if someone asks them tough questions about their position. The opposite is true with performers. Everything about their success is genuine. When you meet them, you meet the embodiment of hard work and success. You meet someone who is confident and assured in their life, their success, and everything else you know about them.

One thing that drives performers to succeed in life is a desire for affirmation. They need attention. However, while other people crave attention because they want it, performers crave attention because they have earned it and believe they deserve it. They have worked hard for it and must be admired and recognized for it.

Typical Action Patterns

It feels good to be loved. For performers, love and affection do not, and should not, come for free. They believe in affection and appreciation only as rewards. You have to do something to deserve the attention you crave, which is why they go the extra mile to succeed.

How do you identify a performer by their actions? Watch closely in your social circle or even at work, and look for the most energetic person amongst you. This is probably a performer. They are quick to start assignments and get impatient when people are slacking on something that they believe can be done much faster. Their lives revolve around succeeding, and they probably have plans in place for how to get from one stage to the next in their pursuit of success. By default, they are go-getters. They are organized and have a meticulous work ethic. They go about their days in order by dealing with one task at a time. Once each is accomplished, they move on to something else and, with the same energy, accomplish that too.

Performers are very good at adapting to a range of situations and environments. While most people might find some changes difficult to handle, they see them as stepping stones towards greater things in life. By adapting to different situations, they are preparing themselves for similar challenges later in life. This is one person who can assume different roles within a short time, and execute them to perfection.

An individual who gets excited about the prospect of success will most definitely be a competitive person, as competition comes naturally to performers. Everything is always a competition in which someone has to come first; and that someone is them. If you beat them at something, rest assured they will go back to the drawing board and try to figure out where they went off the rails. They will never stop until they find a way to get back on top.

There is a good reason why most performers end up as leaders. They have all the qualities any organization wants in a leader, and are driven by the pursuit of success. It follows that everyone who works for them must meet the same standards or get out. To a performer, you are either pulling your weight or out of the team. You are only as good as your contribution, so without that, they can easily replace you with someone else. What else is good about their leadership qualities? Well, they dress the part too.

Typical Thinking Patterns

Performers are a competitive group. The flipside of competition is that for someone to win, someone else has to lose, and performers tend to take loss personally. It feels like they are not good enough, and they will push their limits to prove otherwise. One of the ways of doing this is by using their losses as a stepping stone for improvement. This also adds to their leadership capabilities.

A leader is someone who recognizes potential and nurtures it. A single failed attempt along the way cannot derail success, so when someone in their team fails, they encourage them to remember the pain that comes with failure. They should use that pain to come back stronger and impress. This is their mantra in life, and since learning from their mistakes has placed them in the position of power, they believe everyone else can do the same too.

The typical thought process of a performer is to conduct themselves as professionals. Most of them struggle to set aside the professional when they get back to their homes, so the structure they run in the workplace is often transferred to their homes in their parenting skills. They rarely act on sentiment. Instead, they need data, actionable data. Data, for an intellectual, can be used to give statistics. Data is reliable because they can read and understand it, and then use it to make informed decisions. Sentiments don't offer the same benefits.

If you engage a performer, you must realize they are probably a few steps ahead already. They take calculated risks and consider all possibilities before they make a decision. This perhaps comes from the experience of their leadership position. It is easy for them to ignore everything non-essential and focus on the possibility of risk and return in any situation.

As much as performers love success, they also love to be associated with it. If they do something good, they have to be recognized for it. They will have put in too much effort to let someone else enjoy the limelight. In fact, many performers will quit a company if they feel their efforts are not being recognized and pursue their career in a different environment that allows them to grow and acknowledges their wins.

The other challenge of interacting with a performer is that most of the time, you end up in a battle of wits without realizing it. They like to pick your brain and ask you why you think the way you do. If they feel your ideas are not aligned to their beliefs, they won't hesitate to drown you in data that disapproves your concept and proves that theirs is right.

Typical Feeling Patterns

Why do many people fear to approach their bosses when they need help with personal matters? It is not because they fear reprimand, but because they feel that their bosses are so detached from anything sentimental, they might rationalize their problems and refuse to grant their pleas. While not true for all bosses, it does strike home for performers.

Performers rationalize their approach to everything. A situation has to be factual, and if you are hoping they will show emotions in their response, you are barking up the wrong tree. While they do feel the same emotions that everyone else feels, they do a good job hiding them can be misconstrued as a weakness. Unfortunately, for most performers, this thought pattern can persist and become a toxic trait, to the point where they may literally call people weak for expressing their emotions.

Performers are confident, probably overconfident. They trust in their abilities more than anyone else around them. They would rather do things their way and fail than do it someone else's way and succeed. Following someone else's method is a challenge to them because they believe that their way should be good enough. They should be the best. Why does someone else know more than they do?

Their enthusiasm also means that they place a high value on influential connections. Since they love success, they love to associate themselves with successful people too. If the chance presents itself, they will stop at nothing just to meet and interact with some of the best minds in their industry. This is a teachable moment for them because they believe that in due time, the student will become the master.

While performers are attuned to success, they are also exposed to the challenges and risks that come with it. Because of this, they can get caught in a moment of madness and lash out. Many performers are livid when pushed to the wall, and struggle to handle their temper. They are also often workaholics.

How to Improve Your Life

Adaptation is a good thing. It helps you fit in and get used to new environments and situations, making your life easier. However, there is a risk of adapting to other people's ideas of the person that they want you to be, to the point where you lose grip on your identity. Acceptance is one of the driving forces behind your desire to adapt, but you must recognize when the cost is too high. Don't lose sight of your core values in order to fit in. Remind yourself what is important to your life, and why.

Your priority in life is to care for yourself first, then everyone else. Never lose sight of this awareness. It is what reminds you of your goals in life, and why you are working so hard. Resist the urge to devote much of your time and resources on things that appear to help others but offer no progressive value to your own personal growth. As you work with other people, try to find your identity in the cooperation, and appreciate the value you bring to the team, even if others don't.

One of your weaknesses is pushing yourself beyond your limits to the point of exhaustion. While your desire to succeed is commendable, of what use is success if you cannot enjoy it? Take breaks, go on holiday, find time to unwind, and do things that take your mind off your regular schedules. You will come back rejuvenated, which will prove to be good for your long-term objectives.

Be genuine in your pursuit of success. Do not overstate your importance in other people's lives. Your personality type can mislead you to a point where you focus more on being impressionable than adding value in your life.

Chapter 10: Enneagram Type 2

In this section, you will see eight good qualities, eight stressors, and eight stress behaviors of Enneagram Type 2.

Mark with a tick which ones apply to you.

Do not overthink; answer honestly and accurately. the more accurately you can answer the easier it will be to find your type

GOOD QUALITIES

2s are giving people. They are warm, gentle and kind-hearted, and move towards people in affection. 2s are also loving people and they give off themselves to relationships that are meaningful to them. They are also pleasant and helpful people, who are dedicated and devoted to those they love and care about.

2s are often the most responsive people to meet your physical needs. They may even know what you need before you know it yourself. They are attuned to other people, and if you break down crying they will probably be the first to hand you a tissue and hold a mirror up so you can stop the mascara from dripping down your face. 2s are your friends who you can always count on, and they intuitively can sense if you are hungry, tired or just want to rest.

2s are helpful people. They genuinely want to be of service and rescue those who are in distress. They are able to quickly step in and save those in need. In organizations, 2s know how everything is run, but often from behind the scenes, supporting the front person. CEOs just can't do without them because they know where everything is, and the roles that everyone in the organization plays. They are the glue that helps the company run smoothly.

Along with 4s, 2s are part of the heart center and are one of the romantics of the Enneagram as they often have a classical view of romance: boy meets girl, he sweeps her off her feet, and they fall madly in love. Romance can also come about from everyday interactions, and if not there are plenty of romance novels or movies that can help evoke fresh emotions of love. On the other hand, 2s are repulsed by cruelty and don't like to watch violent programs or horror movies on TV.

2s are empathetic; they intuitively know what others are feeling, what they need, and what they want. If you have fallen over and hurt your leg, they will instinctively know how to take care of you. They know what to say or do, they know how to make you feel comfortable. They are compassionate and for them, it is better to give than to receive.

2s are gifted at connecting with others. They love making new connections with people and they also thrive from connecting people who don't know each other together. At a social event, what a 2 would look forward to is all the good connections they could be making, and all the interesting people they could meet there.

2s are likable people who instinctively know how to please others. They can sense just how different people are, and they know exactly what an individual needs to see or hear. 2s have the intuitive ability to act in a way that can cheer someone up or say something nice that can warm someone's heart.

2s are most sensitive to relationships though, and they enjoy being close to someone whether it is as their special friend or partner. They know how to build people up, nurture them and bring out their strengths. 2s spend a considerable amount of time on their relationships, whether it is with their family, old friends or investing their time and energy in cultivating new friendships. They have the most positive outlook out of the three heart types (2, 3, and 4).

ENNEAGRAM TYPE 2 STRESSORS

2s are overburdened by needing to meet everyone else's needs. 2s believe if they are not kind, and giving they will not be loved. Their heart is their center of intelligence and all information is interpreted through their heart. Like with the other heart types, they are emotionally in tune with the feelings of the room. If you ask a type 2 how other people are feeling, they would know. They have an intuitive sense of picking up that.

When the world of a 2 is not as it should be here are some of the thoughts and beliefs that can pop into their minds and cause them stress.

"I'm not needed"

"I have to keep caring and giving to others"

"I have to save you"

"I can't be separated from you"

"Others needs must be met before mine"

"I must be indispensable"

"I must make you happy"

"After all I've done, I'm not appreciated"

STRESS BEHAVIORS

Here are some of the Type 2 Stress behaviors. Mark with a tick which one applies to you.

2s start to over-give and go overboard in helping others, giving them things they don't need. They feel proud of being indispensable, and they offer to do extra work and juggle many tasks. 2s feel they must hug, warm, and love other people first, and make sure their needs are all met before meeting their own. But they end up devaluing themselves, hoping for just a small amount of attention from those they are helping.

As a result, 2s become spent and worn-out. They lose themselves in giving to others. They volunteer to help others in their projects, listen to them, and help them with chores. In return they may expect excessive appreciation and help for their actions and become resentful when they don't receive the kind of love they want, becoming a martyr.

2s have a general tendency to move towards others to help them. They are not aware of their own limits or their own needs and say 'Yes' to helping others. In doing so, their own needs are repressed and denied. They'll want the last slice of cake but will save it and give it to you instead. They need to have something to give you in exchange for your love.

Because of all the 2 has done for others; they can act entitled and proud of their privileged position. They fantasize about being loved and admired, like a prince or princess. But when they aren't treated well, they may throw a tantrum or sulk.

2s have the ability to adapt to whoever the other person would like or love. They can change into that person like a chameleon. As a result, they do not necessarily know who they are; deep down they have fooled both others and themselves. This confusion can damage a relationship as for there to be a healthy relationship their real self needs to emerge.

2s flatter people in order to be liked and approved of by them. When their attention is on others, their own uniqueness does not shine through. They are not in touch with how they genuinely feel about the person and get caught in relationships where the need for the approval of the other person affects their words and actions.

2s seduce others through charm and generosity, or by appearing childlike. They don't know what they need so they cannot state so directly. Instead, they hope the other will meet their needs. They promise whatever they might need to promise to get someone's attention, but once they have captivated someone, they may not necessarily follow through on their commitments.

2s are drawn to relationships with people who they feel they can 'fix'. They often enable others, which allows the other person not to take responsibility for their actions or shortcomings. They pick up their poop after them. 2 are often caught in codependent relationships where addictive or destructive behavior is overlooked.

TEST RESULTS

Here's how you interpret your Enneagram Test Results.

Scoring (one point for each tick):

Good qualities: 0 – 8

Stressors: 0 -8 (divide by 2)

Stress behaviors: 0 - 8

Divide your stressors score by 2, and add to your good qualities and stress behaviors scores for a total of 0 - 20.

A result of **12 or more** means you identify strongly with the Enneagram Type 2. It could either be your core type (2), your wing (1,3), or you could be connected to the type by a line (4,5,8).

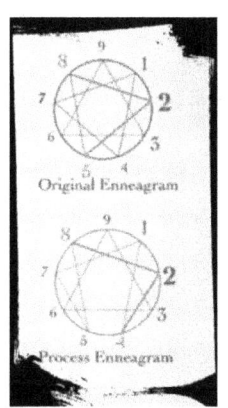

Chapter 11: How To Choose Career Path And A Partner Based On The Kind Of Personality

THE REFORMER

The Reformer is all about control and discretion. She is into sanity and clears arrangements of tips yet not at a frightening Spock kind of manner; she simply prefers to perform in situations that allow her to utilize her nice tender loving attention and critical thinking abilities. She also cherishes employments that provide her a sensible notion of if she is working.

Requires: To be good, to have uprightness and parity

Fears: Becoming malevolent, blemished

Inspiration: To enhance everything, and recognize that a Perfect world

Self-advancement Hints: Be unconstrained and blissful -- love life! Release yourself again and again and again pardon yourself to your own slip-ups

What Kind of Employment?

Search To get something which is

- Practical and Concrete
- Permits You to Earn construction from confusion
- Focus on perfect execution and Lack of missteps

Conceivable Fantasy Jobs: Attorney, cash related organizer, Legislation, Management Executive, Environmental Science, Politics, Social Advocacy main, house plan writer, some type of official who understands what.

Probably Nightmare Jobs: Enhance satire class instructor, kindergarten teacher, busker, barkeep, any action which needs adaptable hours plus a casual kind of mindset towards life.

THE HELPER

Warm, Attractive, compassionate -- The Helper is the person you have to get located beside a very awkward evening gathering. Her heart is tremendous, and her fascination with the lifestyles of different people is certified -- making it important that she does not end up at a vocation that jobs her shine or conducts her sense of empathy worn out. Fulfilling different people satisfies her, which is why any action that involves always ignoring others will make mincemeat of her heart.

Requires: To be loved

Fears: Becoming dishonourable of affection, undesirable

Inspiration: To be loved, required and recognized, and express affections for others

Self-improvement Hints: Try to become progressively self-sustaining and really aware.

What Kind of employment?

Search To get something which will let you

- Influence other people in the backdrop, At a positive posture

- Have plenty of touch with folks
- Give helping others aware Treatment of many others

Conceivable Fantasy Jobs: Assignment, adviser, expert, salesman, advertising pro, barkeep, blogger/vlogger, counsellor attribute author.

Plausible Nightmare Jobs: Tax examiner, college lunches official, operator (subjective, casting, sports, or something else), editorial supervisor.

THE ACHIEVER

Your Companion, who, by one manner or another, figured out how to change weaving to a concentrated game? That's the Achiever. The Achiever is not a yank -- she only has a sense of inherent aggressiveness, also feels her best when she realizes she is faking to be in the maximum stage of her match. A vocation that empowers her to advance up a clearly portrayed stepping stool by way of diligent work will continue to keep her joyful than a lot of the conspicuous substance that goes for "dream jobs" -- and when her competitive demands are kept noise and bolstered on the job, she could be inclined to a manner or another changing your day Buffy gorge to a struggle ("Who do you think was the greatest Buffy beau? The right answer is Spike, and here is why...").

Requires: To feel significant and valuable

Fears: Becoming unworthy

Self-advancement Hints: Try to become progressively pleasant and concentrated on others. Be simple with yourself as well as some other folks about how you feel. Be certain that you take breaks and unwind.

What Kind of job?

Search To get something which will let you

• Work together with other Men and Women who have high Respect from the public stadium

• Watch aftereffects of your projects and receive recognition

• Watch clear progression openings

Conceivable Fantasy Jobs: Attorney, expert (sports, Profession, recreation, or something else), news writer, manufacturer.

Probably Nightmare Jobs: Freelance essay, conducting an Etsy store, any separate work conditions which are more about freestyle career development compared to apparent development.

THE INDIVIDUALIST

The Individualist is cosmetic, delicate, and maybe only a bit unpredictable. She yells performing work that pulls in her capability for self-articulation, and for her, the meticulous work of a having an ingenious vocation off the floor could possibly be warranted, despite all of the trouble -- the struggle of getting by using a not precisely verify employment might feel easy and windy to her, even though a secure gig with benefits in the world's third most significant pencil maker may truly create her vibe like she's passing (that the Individualist should recall this whenever her people try to disclose to her "visiting grad school is essentially a similar matter as turning into a specialist essayist!")

Requires: To earn a character,' get themselves.'

Fears: Being without character or essentialness

Inspiration: To communicate what needs to be, create and encircle self together with excellence, maintenance for ardent needs

Self-improvement Hints: Do matters if you 'feel like' them or not. Abstain from getting long fanciful talks. Exercise normally and endeavour to acquire a regular moving.

What Kind of employment?

Search For something with

- deep significance and motive
- Permit You to communicate what needs be in Creative manners

- Nothing definitive, or about authorizing rules

Conceivable Fantasy Jobs: Therapist, founder, craftsman, yoga instructor, beautician, tattoo craftsman, masseuse, experimental writing teacher.

Probably Nightmare Jobs: Stockbroker, cop, legal counsel, anything else regulatory or focused on implementing another individual's indicators or criteria.

THE INVESTIGATOR

You Know your companion that needs to understand it on your new phone, your new accomplice, the brand-new condos they are working over the street from your house, and the War of 1812? That would be the Investigator. This cerebral sort wishes to chug data such as fine wine and I'm sure the Investigator has a distinct favourite vintage of wine she would enjoy her excitement for studying to be contrasted with. She might not understand it all she intensely wants, but she gets the hang of all that she could on her overall environment.

Requires: To be skilful and capable

Fears: Becoming useless, unfit, or vulnerable

Inspiration: To have advice and understanding of the planet.

Self-advancement Hints: stay related to the physical universe through care, and start adding to other men and women.

What Kind of job?

Search To get something which will enable you to

- Raise Your insight
- Pursue a topic that interests you.
- Have a significant degree of self-rule
- Use realities
- Avoid customer care or client confronting jobs

Conceivable Fantasy Jobs: Anything technician, from program and game strategy to actual construction, expert, examiner, writer, teacher, chief.

Probably Nightmare Jobs: Publicist, server, barkeep, retail labourer, any type of job at which folks regularly ream you out over things that are not actually your issue.

THE LOYALIST

The Loyalist enjoys things the way they are, irrespective of if she does not care for the real items that are, they are. The Loyalist is a worrier, that's why she has never been catfished or missing a massive quantity of money gaming; it is similarly why she might encounter trouble leaving a vocation which makes her troubled nevertheless gives incredibly clear assistance and structure. The Loyalist is your trip or passes companion because seven times after you met her, and moves on her adoration for you by means of stressing. She moves on joy, difficulty, fatigue, and occasionally, gassiness throughout stressing. She's an Ativan. You could get to your airplane ride tomorrow.

Requires: To be protected and strengthened

Fears: Being without assistance and leadership

Inspiration: To fight uncertainty and uneasiness.

Self-advancement: Attempt to be accessible with your tension and uneasiness and comprehend cynicism. Work to be also helpless and trusting in your relations.

What Kind of job?

Search For something with the open doorway for

- Problem-fathoming
- Managing hazard
- Expressing faithfulness, being Bolstered and protected
- Nothing that includes a Whole Lot of danger taking

Conceivable Fantasy Jobs: Writer, teacher, examiner, college instructor, stand-up entertainer, funnies craftsman, dissident, or anything at which she could make something positive from spontaneous stress.

Plausible Nightmare Jobs: Investment financier or another type of job that needs being agreeable always going out on a limb (especially the kind of risks that may irritate different people at her).

THE ENTHUSIAST

You Have to get located by a Helper in a dreadful evening gathering, however, who would you prefer to stay beside in a mixture rave/vaudeville appear/16 class gourmet tasting menu dinners held at a metro subway station? The Enthusiast (who, how about we're real, brought you together to the as her along with one).

This is the companion that makes distinct companions where she belongs, is full of fresh experiences, and, after, through the development of deflecting happenstances, spent Thanksgiving in Pitbull's house in Miami. The Enthusiast needs a job that may bolster her appetite for new experiences, cash in on her get-up-and-go for dwelling, rather than squash her with its bluntness.

Requires: To be content and fulfilled, have prerequisites fulfilled

Fears: Being denied and in misery

Inspiration: To take care of chance, abstain from passing up a significant opportunity, and stay energized and rested in

Self-improvement Hints: operate at seeing your driving powers, rather than surrendering to them. Be consistent; great open doorways return — select quality over the amount on your experiences.

What Kind of employment?

Search To get something which includes

- Creativity and growth
- Difficult circumstances that go Past habitual justification
- Not too restricted or condemned
- Novelty
- Prevent anything with a continuous daily Clinic and formality

Conceivable Fantasy Jobs: Travel essayist, barkeep, onscreen personality, film taker, DJ, audio promotion pro, life coach, entrepreneur, personality writer, health professional, pub proprietor.

Plausible Nightmare Jobs: Client management rep, bookkeeper, legal counsel, expert, or anything else that's tied in with maintaining up a predictable day daily program (and comprises huge quantities of workplace work).

THE CHALLENGER

In Case you are a Challenger, you kind of knew it before you took the exam, is not that so? The Challenger would like to be the main, however not on the grounds that she is hung up on insignificant power excursions -- she just wants the self-sufficiency and chance of never having a whole lot of different managers breathing down her throat. What is more, actually, nobody should inhale her throat down -- employments which have a supervisor always compact scale overseeing are dreadful news for people who are as strong, self-indulgent, and unequivocal since the Challenger.

Requires: Self-insurance, command of your destiny

Fears: Being constrained by other people, being hurt

Inspiration: To behave obviously determined, demonstrate your calibre, and stay accountable for

Self-improvement: Let's have their leadership now and then. Limit the sum you rely upon additional individuals and do not estrange them being surrounded by good individuals makes you more grounded.

What Kind of employment?

Search For something where you could

- Function as chief
- Get items levelled
- Have effect over results
- Fight bad shape

- Prevent jobs with no development Possible, or where you are going to be micromanaged

Conceivable Fantasy Jobs: Manager/executive of supplies, head of vulnerability, independent strategist, financial counsellor, legislator, realtor or programmer, encouraging executive, advertising executive, head of virtually anything.

Plausible Nightmare Jobs: Retail perform free of development potential, whatever includes being closely watched and rounding a great deal of insignificant busywork (such as most passing degree business employments -- do not worry, you will get improved shortly, Challenger!).

THE PEACEMAKER

The Companion who had the choice to convince you to not fight that individual at incidental pub information who obtained by secretly seeing his phone? That's the Peacemaker. Hopeful and eager, the

Peacemaker accepts that people do not all need to behave as buttocks face only to endure. She also accepts that individuals have a natural limitation with respect to goodness, and she could not care less distancing sceptical men and women can come across that. She knows who she actually is, that's why she could be chill about each other individual. She might likewise function as a lone companion that never needed a screen name such as "DARKNESSREIGNS" in secondary school.

Conceivable Fantasy Jobs: Therapist, HR main, arbiter/instructor, editorial director, extremist, non-benefit executive, societal expert, innovativeness mentor, essayist, teacher, youth group pioneer.

Plausible Nightmare Jobs: Attorney, speculation financier, whatever needs being strong to the purpose of estranging others.

Chapter 12: The Investigator

The investigator's growth line runs from point five to point eight while its stress line runs from point five to point seven. The primary words used to describe the investigator, who is also referred to as the observer and the specialist, are innovative, isolated, perceptive, and secretive. Some popular investigator personalities are Siddhartha Gautama Buddha, Stephen Hawking, Vincent van Gogh, Tim Burton, and Kurt Cobain ("Type Five," n.d.).

What is the Investigator?

The biggest desire of a type five personality is to be knowledgeable and skillful. The biggest fear for an investigator is to be perceived as useless and incapable. Investigators are able to focus on very detailed and complicated tasks and tend to be insightful. They are also very curious and can become preoccupied by their thoughts and the situations around them. The biggest motivators for a type five personality are learning, being able to defend themselves from society with their knowledge, and being able to understand the environment and people around them ("Type Five," n.d.).

Investigators are the personality type who want to find out the truth. They not only want to learn the truth, but they want to know the in-depth version of the truth. They want to know every detail, why something happened, when it happened, and how it happened. Unfortunately, this can also cause investigators to think that they can never fully function in today's society. In fact, they can become more withdrawn because they are afraid of what is going to happen ("Type Five," n.d.).

Of course, this feeling is only escalated because type five personalities believe they can't accomplish tasks like other people can. They don't often possess the strong self-confidence that most other personalities do, which can often hold them back from becoming successful.

For investigators to fully understand why something is happening, they have to be able to observe it. They will then take the time they need to understand what they saw, heard, and why it happened. They are critical thinkers and will take the time they need in order to reach a conclusion. Of course, this can cause issues when it comes to deadlines and communicating with other people. This can often make people think that investigators procrastinate. However, they don't often procrastinate like most other personalities do. Instead, they are just taking their time so they can learn what happened and reach their own conclusion ("Type Five," n.d.).

Because of their observation and critical thinking skills, type five personalities are often creating and inventing new things. Because they want to see how things work, they are able to take something apart, put it back together, or create something new. These skills make investigators feel confident as they start to believe they can make their own place in this world. At the same time, their need to observe, learn, and create can often cause them to become more withdrawn from society. While they are fine with having a select group of friends, they do tend to feel lonely ("Type Five," n.d).

One of the biggest struggles for investigators is they don't like to face their problems head on. Because of this, they often have trouble forming relationships and in general struggle with functioning in society, especially within groups of people. In fact, one of the biggest obstacles investigators can face is having to accomplish a task in a team. They are much better at performing tasks individually ("Type Five," n.d.).

Levels of Integration

Healthy Levels

The healthiest level for an investigator is level one. Type five personalities who reach this level are open-minded. They also tend to be pioneer investigators. They will often spend their time figuring out new ways to accomplish tasks.

A level two can gain a lot of insight through everything they experience in their life. They have a strong ability to concentrate on tasks but can become too drawn into the task and can cause them to lose sight of what they needed to originally do. They are very observant, mentally alert, and good at predicting what will happen in the future because of their observational skills (Cloete, n.d.).

A level three will always look for something new to learn. They will often become an expert in their field of study, are highly independent, and skillful masters (Cloete, n.d.).

Average Levels

An investigator at a level four will often try to find new ways to do something. They will view things as a challenge, which will in turn help them to absorb the information they want to learn. They are often busy gathering as many resources as they can, so they can increase their knowledge. It is around this level where the investigator starts to become in-tune with their skills and works on ways to master their talents (Cloete, n.d.).

A level five will start to fall victim to their fantasy world. While they remain curious and continue to expand their knowledge, they also become detached from the things they learn and the ideas this knowledge puts into their head. It's during this phase that they start to focus more on dark topics, which can contribute to their increasingly morbid thoughts as they get trapped within their mind (Cloete, n.d.).

An investigator at level six is deemed argumentative and pessimistic. While they continue to learn, they don't focus on growing their knowledge like investigators do in the healthy level or the higher average levels. A type five personality would rather not have people interfere with their thoughts and tend to withdraw from society (Cloete, n.d.).

Unhealthy Levels

A level seven investigator is not only aggressive but highly unstable. They are victims of their dark thoughts, which often leads them to become repelled by other people. As a result, they become increasingly isolated from society (Cloete, n.d.).

An investigator who is at a level eight starts to become horrified by their increasingly dark thoughts. While they continue to dive into these thoughts, they become frightened by them and often realize that they are unhealthy. However, most do their best not to focus on how shockingly horrible their thoughts are as they become progressively obsessed with them (Cloete, n.d.).

The unhealthiest level for an investigator is a level nine. At this point, a type five personality will often suffer a psychotic break. They are often diagnosed with various mental disorders such as schizophrenia (Cloete, n.d.).

Subtypes of the Investigator

Social Category is Totem

One reason a type five personality is called the investigator is that they often carry characteristics that are associated with investigators. People who fit this personality type tend to look into the details of situations around them. They want to know why something happens and how it happened. They will often do their own research or talk to people in order to find out what is going on. They don't tend to listen to what other people say, partially because they are also known to disconnect themselves from other people. By disconnecting themselves, they are able to better manage their emotions and thoughts, which can help them have a clear mind when they are learning (Cloete, n.d.).

Self-Preservation Category is Castle

Investigators are believed to be introverts because they tend to withdraw from society. They keep close to a small number of friends, and they like to remain in their home as this helps keep their social boundaries clear. At the same time, they can often be seen observing people and situations as they try to figure out what is going on around them and why. Their need to be left alone in their home can often create a negative effect because they can find themselves protecting their privacy at an intense degree, which makes it hard for them to let their guard down if they need help from others or if people want to socialize with them (Cloete, n.d.).

One-on-One Category is Confident

Investigators will feel a lot of compassion and become very passionate towards a couple of people in their private life. However, this can help them to thrive socially, or it can cause them to test their partner or friends to make sure that they will not be harmed or betrayed by them. A type five personality might test their partner because they are afraid of letting their guard down. At the same time, investigators can become overly protective of their partner because they don't want to share this person with anyone else (Cloete, n.d.).

Relationships with Other Types

Like with the other personalities, investigators can get along with any type of personality. However, they are more compatible with type three personalities and less compatible with type two. Any personality that a type five gets to know can help them thrive or in other cases, cause more struggles. However, because a type five is typically non-confrontational, they won't often express how they feel. Instead, they will start to withdraw from people and society as a whole ("Relationships (Type Combinations)," n.d.).

Wing Types

One wing type for the investigator is a type four, also known as the individualist. Type four can help type five find a balance within their life, especially when it relates to how passionate they become about certain people. Other strengths include connecting with others, learning how to connect their emotions to their thoughts, and connecting themselves to their intuitions. The challenges that the investigator faces due to this wing type include becoming attached to fantasies, becoming depressed because they feel misunderstood by society, and withdrawing further away from society to avoid confrontation (Cloete, n.d.).

The second wing type for the investigator is a type six personality. The strengths that type six brings to type five include being able to understand someone else's point of view, increasing their connection with groups of people, and increasing their self-confidence so they become more comfortable in social settings. The challenges that a type five may experience from a type six are becoming more socially withdrawn because they believe they can't trust people and think that they will upset people if they continue to be overly social (Cloete, n.d.).

Center Points

If you have a type five personality, you are a part of the head center (Cloete, n.d.). You think that you have to know everything about the situation before walking into it. Therefore, you will often observe everything about what is going on, so that you know exactly what to expect.

Type five's strengths:

- **Intellectual**
- **Dependable**
- **Self-reliant**
- **Calm**
- **Thoughtful**
- **Respectful**

Type five's weaknesses:

- **Overthinking**
- **Hoarding**
- **Isolation**
- **Detached**

How to Grow Personally

Learn to Relax

Investigators often struggle with learning to relax. This can make them more intense, which can cause them to withdraw from people because they don't want to cause any problems, especially since they also don't like confrontation. Therefore, type five personalities need to take extra care to make sure they are able to unwind and find something, such as a hobby, that will help them relieve some of the stressors in their life. For example, going out for a walk, riding a bicycle, or joining a gym are great ways to relieve stress. However, some investigators are highly creative, which means that they might be able to relieve their stress through art or writing (Cloete, n.d.).

Avoid Distractions

Type five personalities are curious about everything, which can cause them to be easily distracted. When this happens, they often forget about the tasks they have to accomplish or else fall behind on them, which leads to the need of an extension on their deadlines or pushing the work aside. Therefore, it is important to make sure you accomplish your tasks, even if it means you need to use self-discipline or find techniques that will help you stop from getting too distracted by situations that aren't as important (Cloete, n.d.).

Don't Get Trapped by Your Thoughts

Because investigators are always thinking and trying to learn new things, they can easily become trapped in their own thoughts. When this happens, they tend to avoid the people around them and further withdraw from society. Because this can make an investigator feel lonely over time, often leading them to depression, it is important to make sure that they schedule social time into their calendar. Even if you only have a few friends, which many personalities are comfortable with, you will still want to make time to go to the movies, go out to eat, or hang out with them and play video games at home. This will help you keep a balance in your life so you don't feel trapped by your thoughts (Cloete, n.d.).

Chapter 13: Ennea-Type Six – "The Loyalist"

Aliases: The Devil's Advocate, The Questioner

The Committed, Security-Oriented type

Generally described as:

Engaging Responsible

High-strung Intuitive

At their best, Type Sixes are described as:

Skeptical Committed

Self-Reliant Humorous

Motto: "The world is a dangerous place. If I avoid making mistakes, I will be safe."

The Loyalist in General

People who exhibit a Core Type Six have a strong desire to live in a "safe" world, and actively work to create a secure environment through relationships and alliances. They place a high priority on duty, while also determining they should choose their own alliances and duties.

Type Six people genuinely desire to defend and protect others, while also being afraid they can't defend and protect themselves.

They are often ambivalent toward authorities, indecisive about big ideas, and seemingly idiosyncratic to others. It is often said about Type Six people that "the opposite is also true." They are a bundle of contradictions.

When a Type Six person can fully engage and express themselves, they become confident leaders, reliable and supportive, tender and empathetic. They enjoy building a group of people who come together and cooperate for a cause. They make excellent team members and project coordinators, as it is naturally easy for them to be organized, proactive, and efficient decision makers.

Sometimes, while a Type Six person is working to develop a sense of security, they become overly cautious and indecisive when they experience anxiety about the "right" thing to do. When they doubt themselves, they also doubt others, which can lead to suspicious, judgmental treatment toward people they don't know and even those they do. Loyalists prefer to be seen as problem solvers, hard workers, and socially adaptable.

When a Type Six person develops a sense of dependability in their world, and trust in their inner guidance and emotions, they feel fulfilled. Their natural drive to feel secure means they create this security for others, becoming the go-to person when something needs to get done. Protecting and providing for others makes a Loyalist feel worthwhile.

How Loyalists See Themselves vs. How Others See Them

Loyalists see themselves as genuinely dedicated to working hard, but they also become resentful that they do too much, or fearful that they're not doing enough. They think they are driven by a true desire to make others feel accepted – truly loyal people – but actually, Loyalists generally operate under the feeling that no one accepts them. They often seek reassurance that they "are enough" and that others won't leave them at the first mistake. While the Loyalist believes that their intelligence makes them more in-tune with their emotions, other people may see the same intelligence as lacking emotion.

Loyalists are highly invested in seeing themselves as the "best" planners. They worry, thinking through issues they believe no one else does, seeing their anxieties as uncommon and perhaps shameful. They think others may not recognize it, but the drive to secure their world causes Type Sixes to become aggressive and angry.

Because Type Sixes are such deep thinkers, they often doubt their own ideas and decisions, which can make them heavily reliant on other people's opinions. Seeking out feedback, they may simultaneously also doubt it, and can even suspect that people are attempting to undermine them with bad advice. With too much reinforcement of this pattern, the Type Six begins to criticize, doubt, and rebuke all opinions from others.

While the Loyalist Ennea-type can see themselves as the embodiment of a mighty, protective warrior – because, in their view, they work hard to make the word better – they can come across as cowardly and paranoid at times. The Loyalist sees themselves as cooperative, while actually preventing group cohesion by being petty or manipulative when their emotions are not being addressed. While Type Sixes may enjoy or find fulfillment in having large networks that recognize their accomplishments, it can be frustrating to others when they begin to see their network's opinions as greater than their own.

The "Average" Loyalist's Mental Health

When Loyalists are at an average level of health, they may feel that they need to organize and make better decisions to bring the security that they seek into their lives. They are detail-oriented and vigilant, but also become demanding and cautious. Sometimes sending mixed messages to others about their needs, decisions can shift with new information. Loyalists at this level of health tend to exhibit passive-aggressive behaviors toward situations that threaten their security, while also priding themselves on being proactive toward problems and able to maintain many relationships at once.

When a Loyalist is feeling better than average, they may be full of the energy to organize, plan, and execute on their goals. They anticipate problems and can help others clearly see solutions to tough situations. At this level of health, a Loyalist wants everyone to see them as reliable and is quick to hand out favors and assistance, but they may also be sensitive, sarcastic, or argumentative.

Moving Toward Integration: Loyalists At Their Best

When moving in their Direction of Integration (growth) and exhibiting their best qualities, Loyalists become accepting, supportive, dutiful, and optimistic and can shed their fear.

Basic Desire(s): To achieve security and support.

Basic Motivation(s): To feel certain and sure, seeks security and support through others, even while testing the bounds of that support.

Unique Gift(s): Warmth, loyalty, imagination, sense of humor.

Basic Goal: To achieve security through careful observation and alertness.

When Loyalist's Mental Health is Excellent

When at their best, Loyalists are trusting and trustworthy, selfless and courageous, optimistic and expressive. They both inspire and lead others, as they realize their interdependence with those in their close circles. Empathetic, intuitive, and thoughtful, they embody self-reliance and self-esteem.

As Type Six people Disintegrate, they become more selfish, less trusting, and less compassionate. Turning inward when they feel their safety is threatened, they begin to question bonds with others and to disconnect from anyone questionable. Although they enjoy and find fulfillment in working with others through positive relationships, they quickly divert energies into the relationships they see as most valuable.

Moving Toward Disintegration: Loyalists When Stressed

When moving in the Direction of Disintegration (stress), the normally relaxed and humorous Loyalist regresses toward becoming competitive and arrogant.

Basic Fear(s): Fears insecurity and anxiety, being alone and/or without guidance

Triggering Emotion(s): **Fear and Doubt**

When Fixated: Becomes cowardly

What Type Six People Might Struggle With

Type Six people can suffer from emotional disconnect and isolation, anxiety that causes them to obsess over small details that ends up pushing people away.

At times, Type Sixes can become so emotionally insecure that they become afraid of everything – "afraid of being afraid." The changing nature of the world can become overwhelming, and they may become paralyzed, preventing from making decisions, connecting with their emotions, and connecting with others. A Type Six person might spend time and energy focusing on the "chaos" and social "disruptions," ignoring the sense of peace they get from their relationships and established place in the world.

Type Sixes tend to overlook or ignore positive feelings and beliefs when under stress and dealing with challenge. Feelings of incompetence, unpreparedness, and disconnect from others can complicate their intense need security.

When Loyalist's Mental Health is Struggling

When fully disintegrated and under stress, Loyalists become paranoid and can lash out, feeling they need to protect themselves from everyone. They can suffer from high anxiety, paranoia, and self-destructive behavior, trying to keep themselves safe by cutting off society.

As Loyalists begin to decrease their stress and focus on higher levels of health, they become welcoming and trusting as they understand that not everyone is "out to get" them. The healthier the Loyalist's mindset, the less they will focus on the need to trust others and focus on the trust that people have already earned from them.

Potential Addictive Struggles

Type Six people might struggle with violent tendencies, "lashing out" at themselves or others when their security is threatened. In some cases, extreme feelings of stress or isolation can contribute to high levels of alcohol abuse, or use of caffeine and other stimulants.

Some Type Sixes may struggle with rigid ideas that impede their health, such as poor nutrition or excessive exercise habits. In order to achieve a feeling of stability, an unhealthy Type Six person may engage in intense levels of self-control with food, substances, or physical requirements.

Overcoming Challenges of the Loyalist Ennea-Type

It's important for the Loyalist to alleviate their anxiety. They feel things deeply, and being so intensely intellectual, can focus on their anxiety, feeling like it's higher than other people's. Which, in turn, increases their anxiety. If a Type Six personality is not working to trust and connect with others, they can become lost in their own fears. Healthy stress relief is essential for the Loyalist to stay balanced and at their best.

Being the Best Loyalist

Harness the best aspects of your Loyalist Ennea-type and diminish negative traits that emerge under stress. If you're a Loyalist, or know someone who is, consider how the following techniques can help you unlock and grow the best version of yourself.

Get Your Emotions Out

Type Six people need to embrace, explore, and come to terms with their anxieties. Sometimes, they can't recognize how their fearful energy can be focused to drive productivity and let them create amazing things. To maintain balance, a Loyalist should learn to listen, hear, and remember others' compliments and positive feedback. Anxiety can grow when they feel isolated, and when they feel they can't trust anyone, they will begin to doubt their own worth even more.

Type Six people find joy in finding a passion to pour their fears and anxieties into – something that they can engage in without judgment, or when the creation is shared, people they trust will support their efforts. By focusing on awareness of their emotional states, they will not be as subject to them, and will be able to maintain more balanced moods and healthier relationships.

Suggestions:

Engage in individual or group therapy, especially those that teach anxiety management and trust-building techniques. Meditate. Paint. Sculpt. Journal. Dance. Go to or perform in stand-up comedy or improv comedy. Exercise (in moderation), especially on a cooperative team.

Establish Peace and Order

Type Six people thrive when their environment supports low levels of anxiety. They are prone to clear, minimal, organized beauty, and when the world feels chaotic, it can reflect in their day-to-day lives. To maintain balance, a Loyalist must learn to be aware and manage their emotions, in their environment as well as their mind.

Type Six people find joy in appreciating the orderly beauty in the world, especially if they can integrate that order into their own lives. Trusting their own instincts and decisions for creating their world can teach them to actively engage with their agency in the world.

Suggestions:

Garden. Schedule regular deep cleaning projects around your home, with your car or bikes, and other often-used items that benefit from regular care. Organize a bookshelf, digital music collection, or other archive. Spend time at a library, aquarium, or museum. Take up a creative, hands-on detail-oriented hobby such as model building, digital photography editing, or knitting.

There are simple things a Loyalist can do to hone their ability to connect with others and their society at large, enhancing their own positivity, especially when they give themselves the freedom to trust their inner peace.

Chapter 14: Enneagram Type 7 - The Dreamer/Epicure

Triad: Type 7 is part of the Mind Triad, with types 5 and 6

Core Belief: the world is exciting and full of opportunities

With this core belief, the Sevens' outlook is very optimistic. They look at possibilities and fun, always eager for new experiences.

They are often described as the Peter Pans' of the world because they can look much younger than their actual age. They are so excited by life's possibilities that they have the zest of young children and it is almost as if their bodies retain this zest as they grow physically older.

At their best, Sevens are visionaries with very active minds that are producing a constant stream of new ideas. They see the global picture and are quick to act.

They have the capacity to excite other people with their ideas and vision. They are confident and charming and can make great leaders. Sevens have an abundance of energy and are always on the move. Their fun, positive 'can do' attitude is infectious and people quickly warm to them. They rarely stay still for long. Sevens are the life and soul of a party. With their quick wit and charm you usually find them entertaining a group.

The downside of always looking for excitement is that Sevens can get bored very easily and quickly. Variety is important to them and they don't like to limit their options by committing to something. You'll often find that, socially, they have many alternatives to choose from, and won't decide until the last minute which one to take - and will often attempt to fulfill more than one! This lack of commitment and easy boredom means that Sevens are great at starting projects, but not so good at finishing them or seeing them through to the end. In a job, Sevens will often move to a new job within 2 years of starting any job.

As with other Mind Triad patterns the Sevens experience fear as a core emotion. Their way of coping with fear is to stay active all the time, because they know that the moment they stop, the fear will rise to the surface. This drives them to be active from the moment they awake to when they finally fall asleep.

They can be positive to the point of being in denial about something not working out in their life or business, until it is too late to do anything about it.

Types 7 tend to believe that the world is full of opportunities and so they spend all their time and energy searching for ways to make life easier. They are highly intuitive people with high energy levels and they find it difficult to relax as they are so absorbed fitting together the pieces of life's puzzle.

Their underlying motivation is a fear of discomfort or pain and they go to great lengths to avoid experiencing these feelings. They are compulsive optimists. There is a solution to every problem - you just have to find it.

From a positive perspective, Types 7 are often visionaries and idealists who may have the means to solve our global problems. They believe that everyone is good at heart even if it takes a machine to dig deep enough to find it. By trusting in their fellow man, they tend to bring out the best in people. They make ideal entrepreneurs as they don't believe in failure and will change tack at a moment's notice if that is required.

But Dreamers often find it difficult to see a project through to the end because they are so focused on having fun and gritting your teeth and grinding out a result is often not much fun. The more successful ones generally employ another personality type to undertake such tasks as they acknowledge their weakness. Dreamers crave pleasure which they get by pursuing new challenges. This personality type has been linked to the "deadly" sin of gluttony as they will feed their addiction to pleasure above and beyond almost everything else.

So do you fit the Dreamer role?

Do you immediately start looking for solutions when you are presented with a problem even if it belongs to someone else?

Can you talk to anyone? Do people seek you out at dinner parties and other social occasions? Were you the most popular kid in school?

Do people often comment on how "gifted" you are?

Tips for dealing with the negative side of the dreamer type:

Make it a specific goal to follow through one task from beginning to the end.

Recognize that having multiple projects on the go at one time can be a way of trying to escape from reality.

Stop thinking that anyone who disagrees with you is criticizing you. Constructive criticism is often useful.

If you find yourself acting eccentrically or living in fantasy, embrace your real life and find reasons to be optimistic and radiate good cheer in life.

Conclusion

The Enneagram is probably one of the most open-ended of personality typing systems, and this is one of the best things about it. However, this does not mean that it uncovers all there is to know about human beings.

The core principle that lead to its development in the first place is that individuals are analyzable only up to a certain point. There are no simple tricks and explanations to how the human heart, mind, and spirit operates. We can only take the Enneagram as a starting point. The patterns it provides will help you take the first steps but you will have to keep going so you can find the profound truth about your true identity and your own place in this world.

This is just a reader's digest version— so much more to learn, and more importantly to implement in your life. Join the enneagram community and try to listen to Enneagram teachers to determine what resonates with you.

Thank you downloading this book. I hope you enjoy your journey.

www.ingramcontent.com/pod-product-compliance
Lightning Source LLC
Chambersburg PA
CBHW070759040426
42333CB00060B/1130